BEAUTIFUL SONGS
FOR ACCORDION

ISBN 978-1-70516-135-7

Visit Hal Leonard Online at
www.halleonard.com

World headquarters, contact:
Hal Leonard
7777 West Bluemound Road
Milwaukee, WI 53213
Email: info@halleonard.com

In Europe, contact:
Hal Leonard Europe Limited
42 Wigmore Street
Marylebone, London, W1U 2RN
Email: info@halleonardeurope.com

In Australia, contact:
Hal Leonard Australia Pty. Ltd.
4 Lentara Court
Cheltenham, Victoria, 3192 Australia
Email: info@halleonard.com.au

ALL OF ME

Words and Music by JOHN STEPHENS
and TOBY GAD

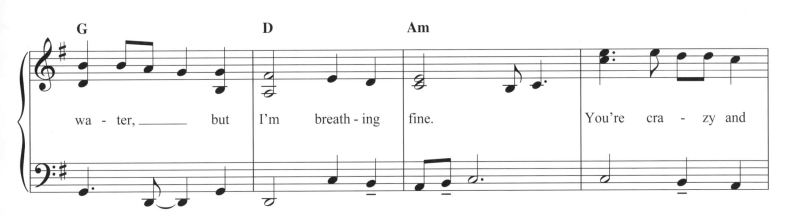

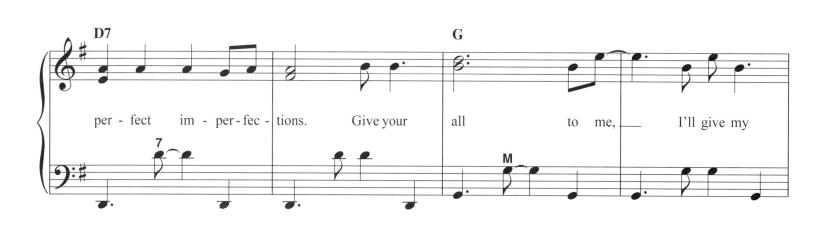

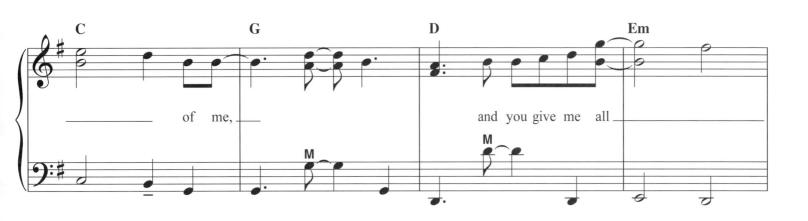

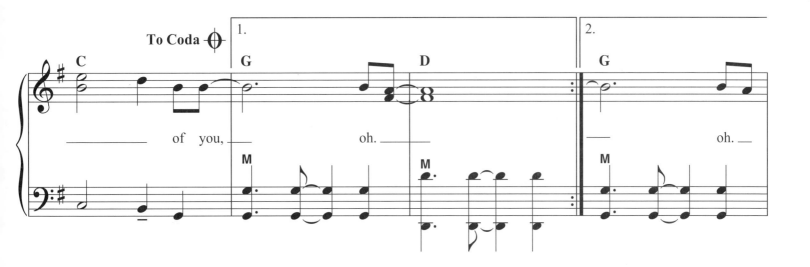

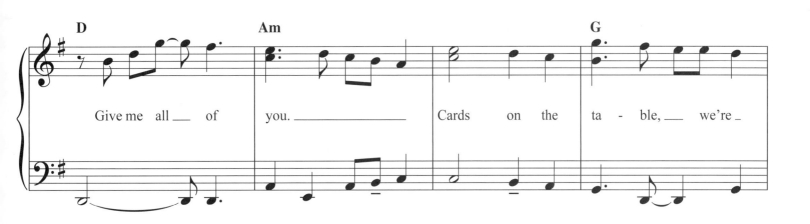

both show - ing __ hearts. __ Risk - ing it all, though __ it's __

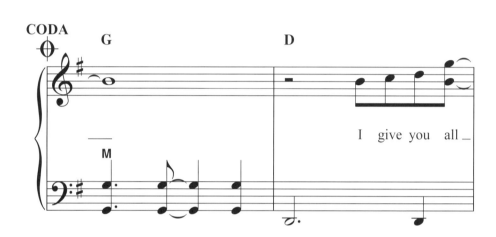

D.S. al Coda

CODA

hard. 'Cause

I give you all __

of me, __ and you give me all __

of you, __ oh. __

CANDLE IN THE WIND

Words and Music by ELTON JOHN
and BERNIE TAUPIN

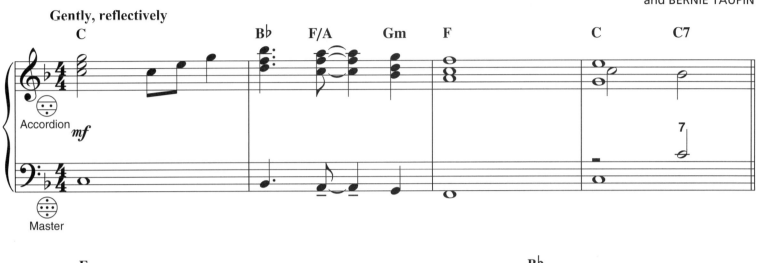

Good-bye, Nor - ma Jean, _____ though I nev - er knew you _____ at all
Lone - li - ness _____ was tough, _____ the tough-est role you ev - er played.

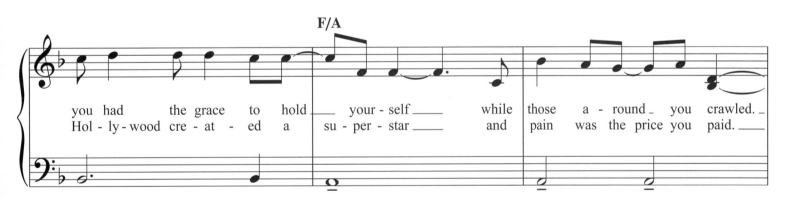

you had the grace to hold _____ your-self _____ while those a - round _____ you crawled.
Hol - ly-wood cre - at - ed a su - per-star _____ and pain was the price you paid. _____

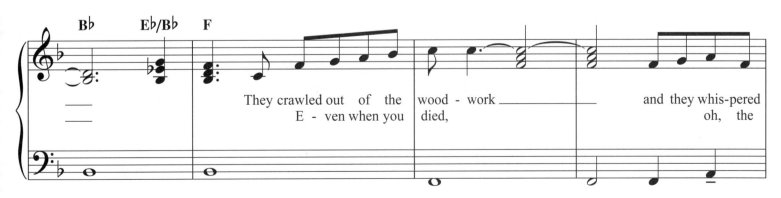

_____ They crawled out of the wood - work _____ and they whis-pered
E - ven when you died, oh, the

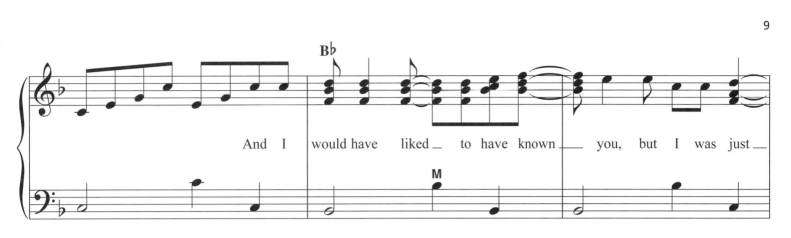

And I would have liked __ to have known __ you, but I was just __

__ a kid. __ Your can - dle burned __ out long be - fore __ your

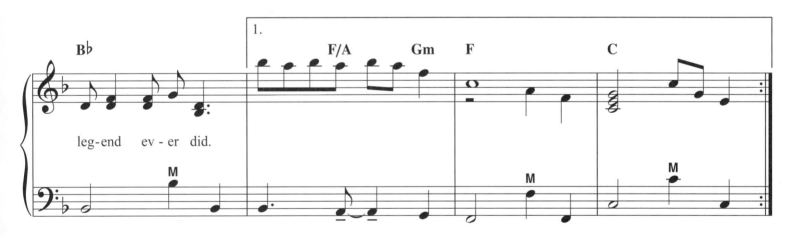

leg-end ev - er did.

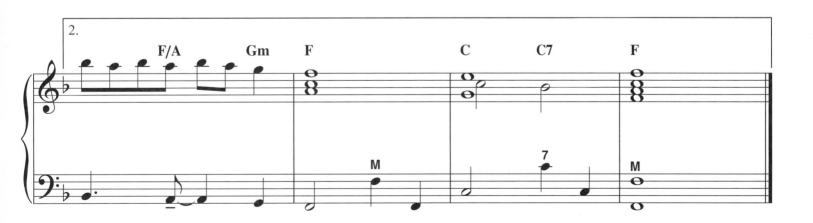

ALWAYS ON MY MIND

Words and Music by WAYNE THOMPSON,
MARK JAMES and JOHNNY CHRISTOPHER

11

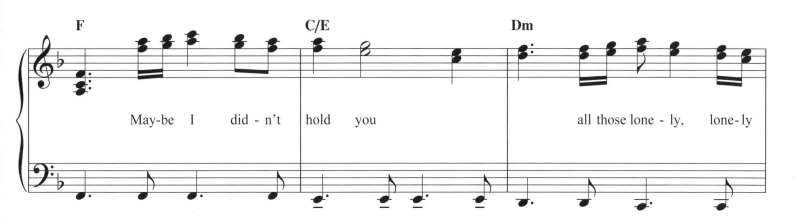

times, __ and I guess I nev-er told you

I'm so hap-py that you're mine. _____ If I made you feel

sec - ond best, __ girl, I'm sor - ry I was blind.

You were al - ways on my mind. You were al - ways on my

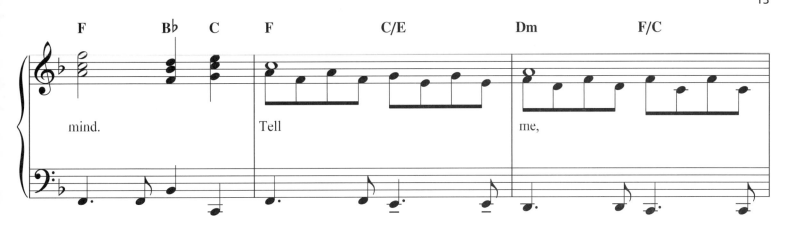

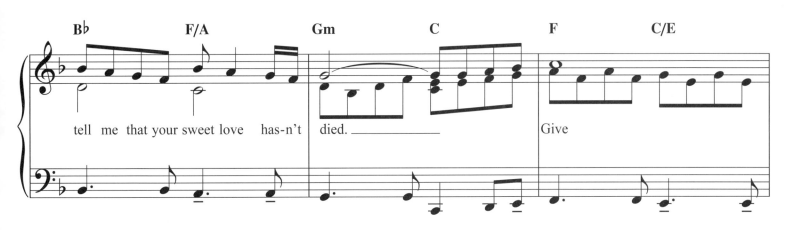

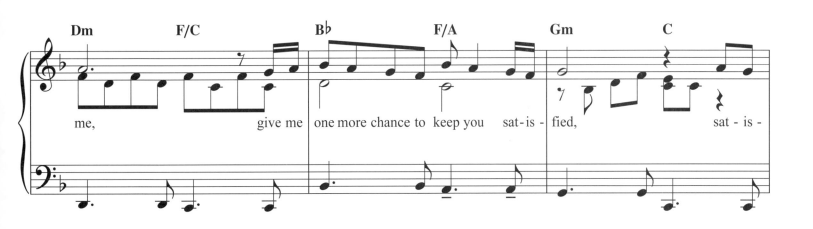

BRIDGE OVER TROUBLED WATER

Words and Music by
PAUL SIMON

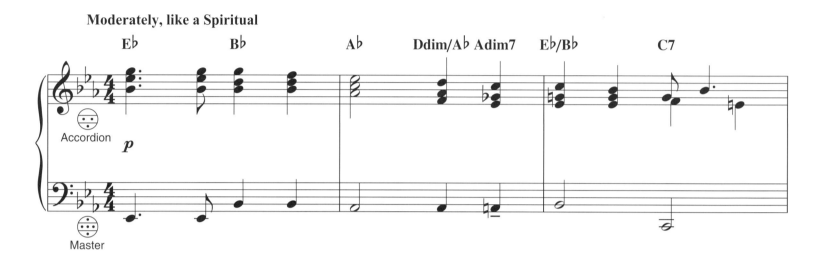

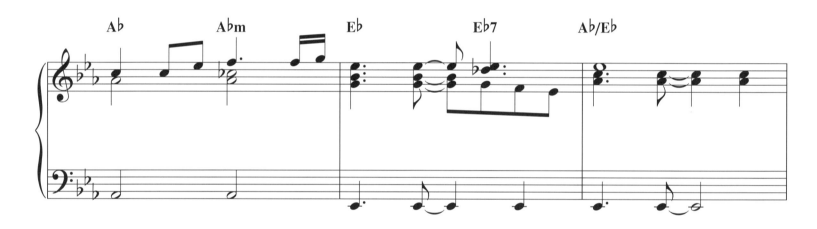

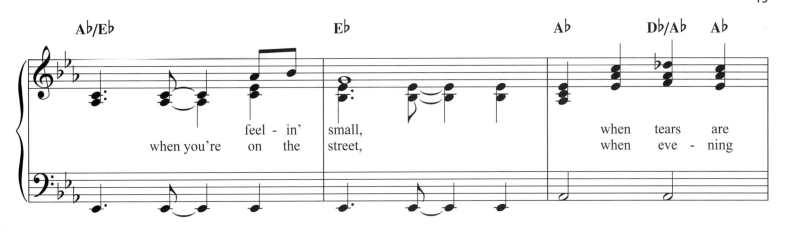

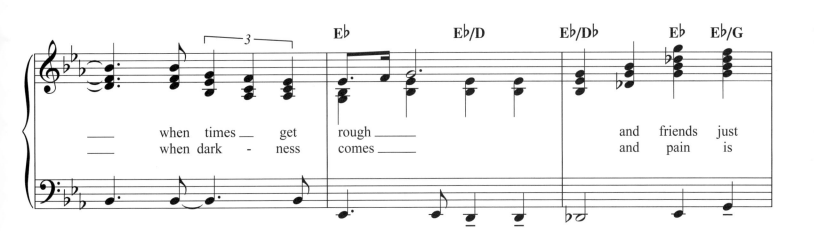

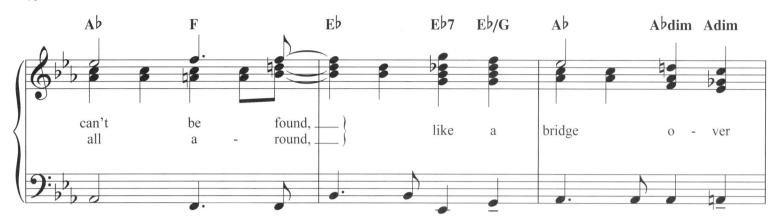

can't   be   found, ____ \}   like   a   bridge   o - ver
all   a - round, ____ \}

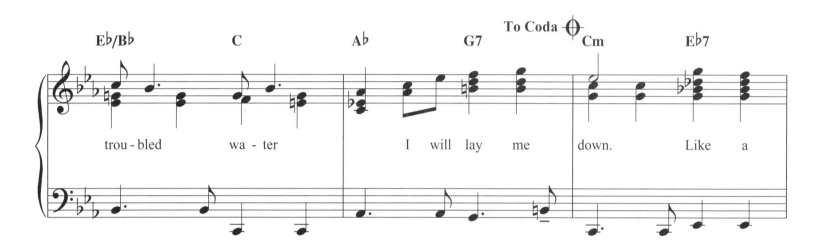

trou - bled   wa - ter   I   will   lay   me   down.   Like   a

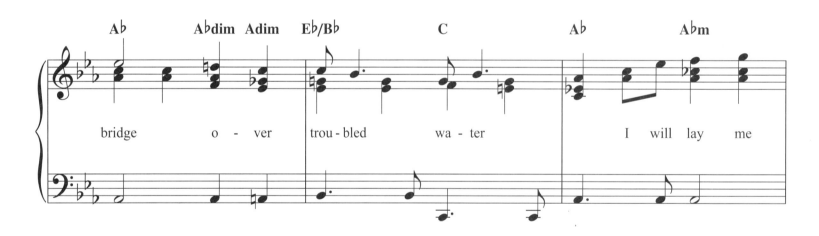

bridge   o - ver   trou - bled   wa - ter   I   will   lay   me

down.

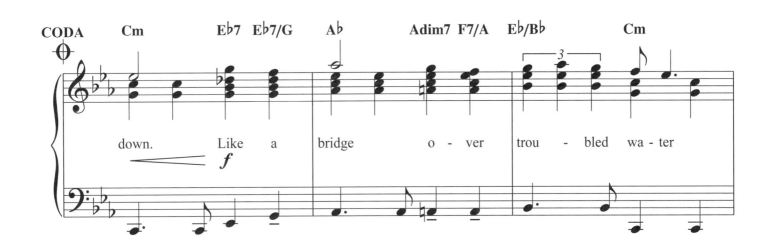

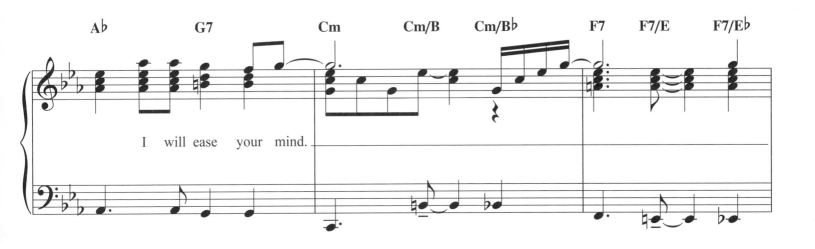

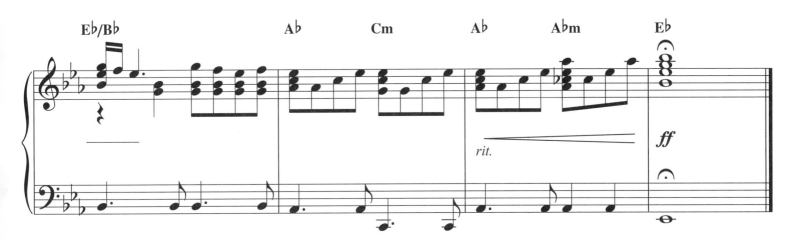

CHARADE
from CHARADE

Music by HENRY MANCINI
Words by JOHNNY MERCER

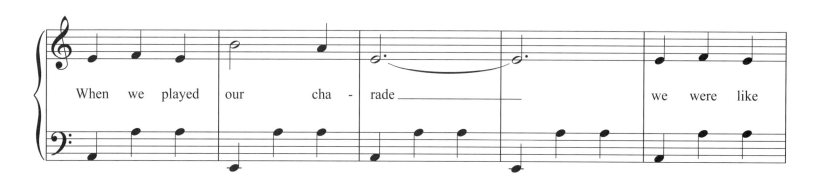

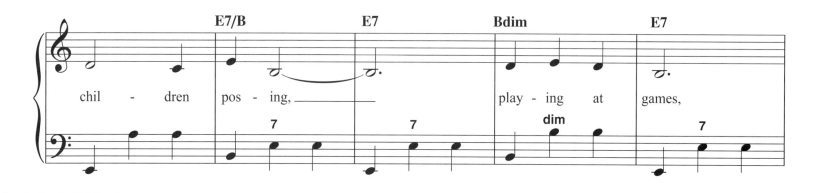

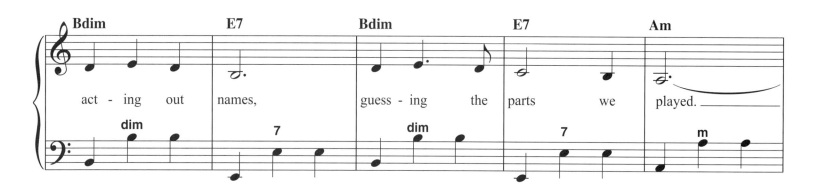

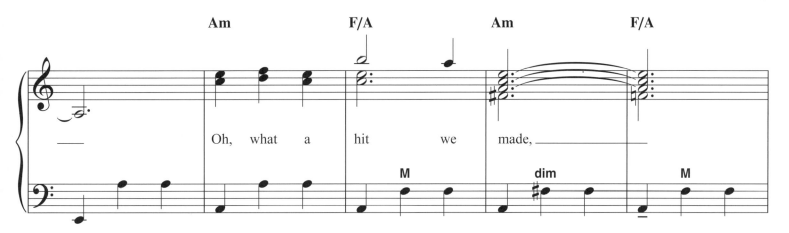

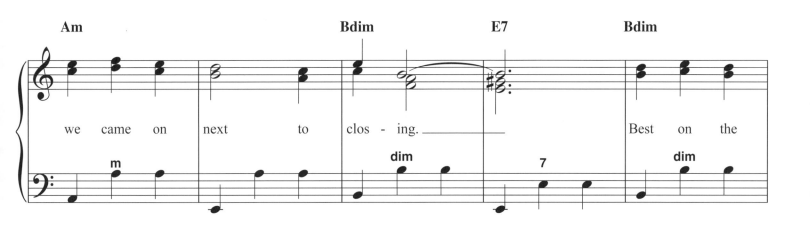

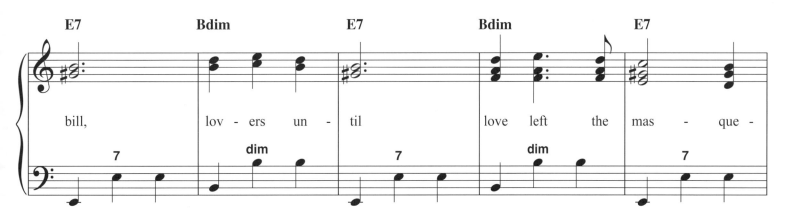

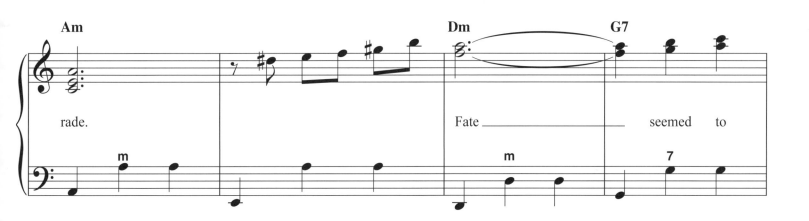

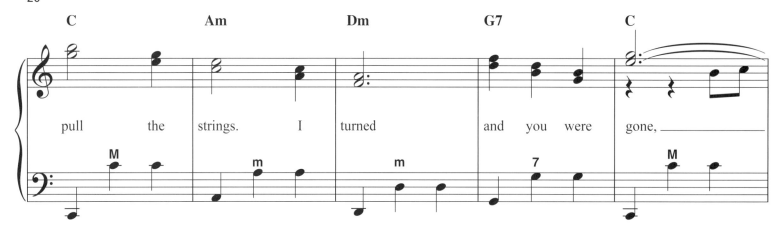

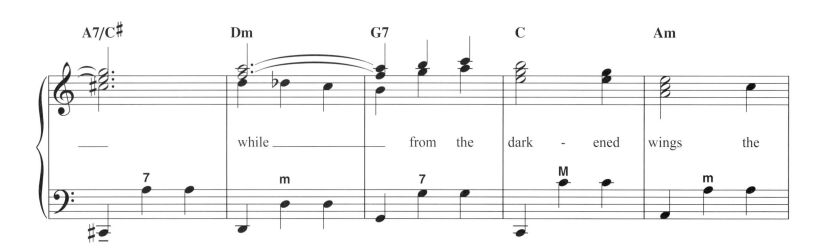

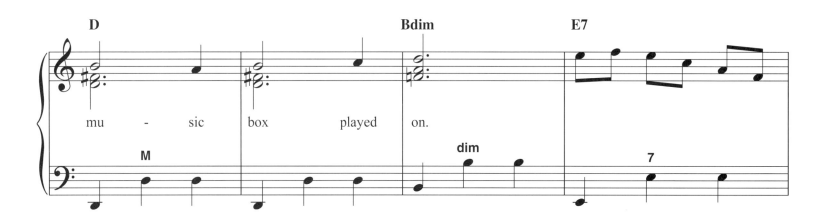

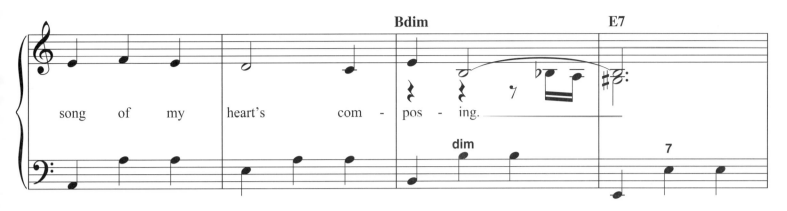

song of my heart's com - pos - ing.

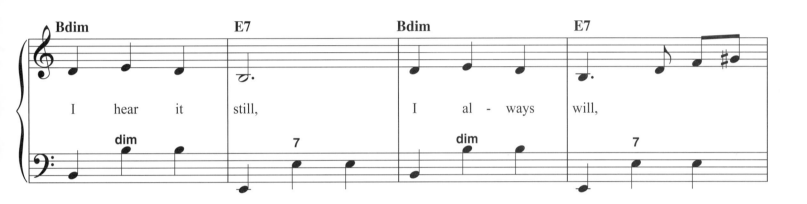

I hear it still, I al - ways will,

best on the bill _____ cha -

rade. _____

(They Long to Be)
CLOSE TO YOU

Lyrics by HAL DAVID
Music by BURT BACHARACH

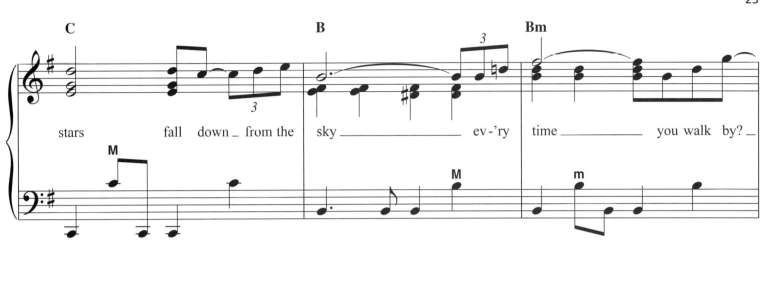

stars   fall   down _ from the   sky _____ ev-'ry   time _____ you walk by? _

___   Just   like   me, ___   they   long   to   be

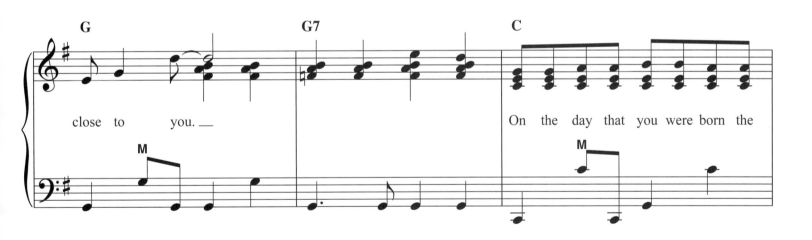

close   to   you. _   On   the   day   that   you   were   born   the

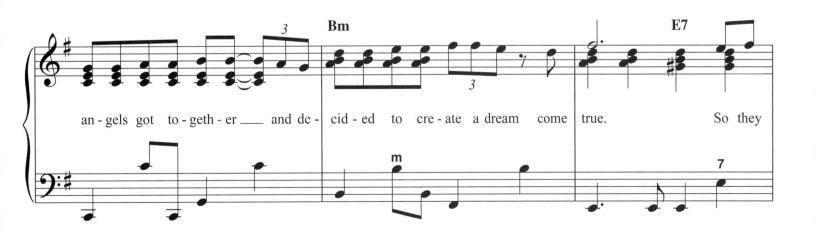

an - gels got to - geth - er ___ and de - cid - ed   to   cre - ate a dream come true.   So they

sprin-kled moon-dust in your hair of gold and star-light in your eyes of blue.

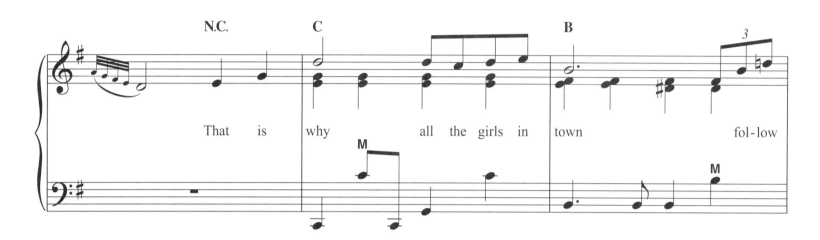

That is why all the girls in town fol-low

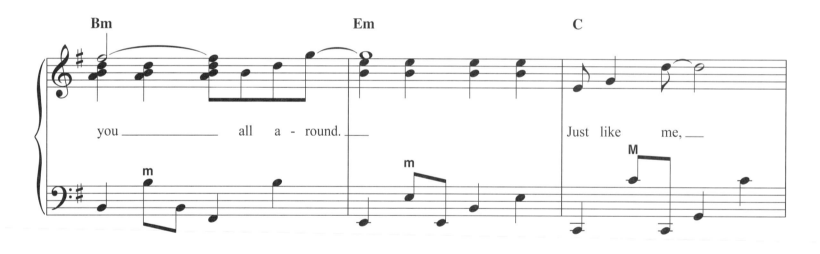

you _____ all a - round. ___ Just like me, ___

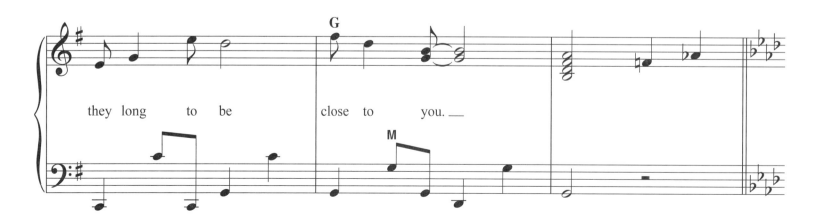

they long to be close to you. ___

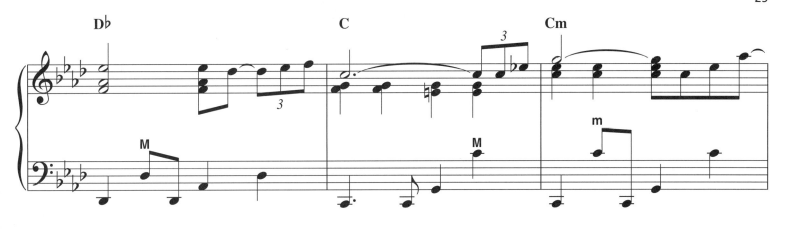

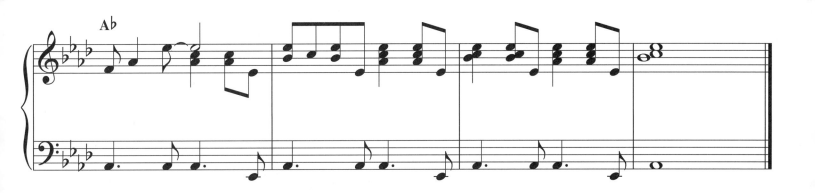

EASY ON ME

Words and Music by ADELE ADKINS
and GREG KURSTIN

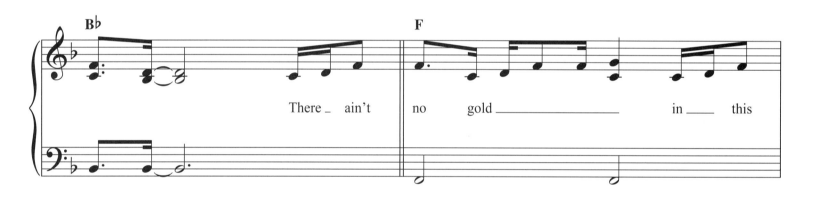

There _ ain't no gold _____ in ___ this

riv - er _____ that I've been wash - ing ___ my ___ hands in for-

ev - er. ___ I know there is hope _____ in ___ these

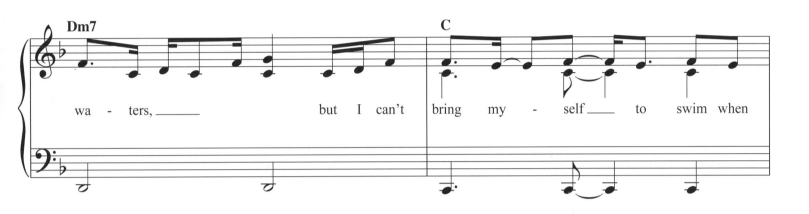

wa - ters, _____ but I can't bring my - self ___ to swim when

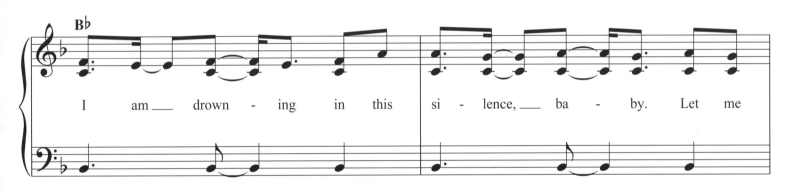

I am ___ drown - ing in this si - lence, ___ ba - by. Let me

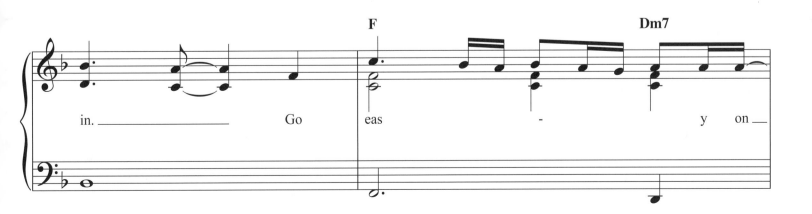

in. _____ Go eas - y on ___

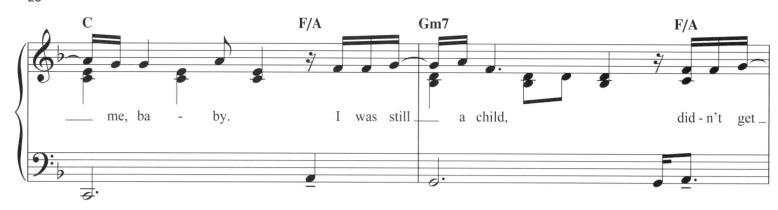

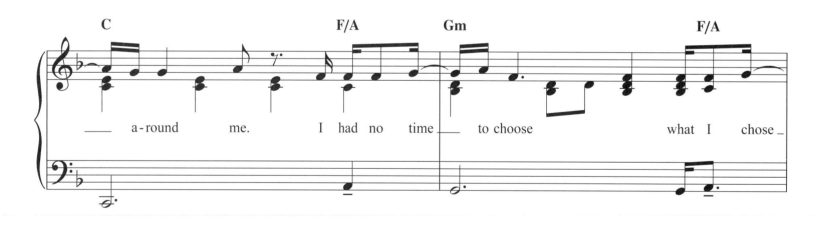

There _ ain't

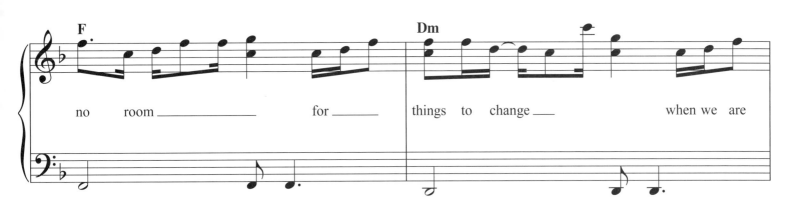

no room _____ for _____ things to change ____ when we are

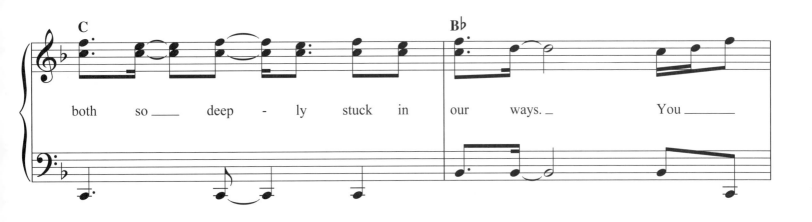

both so ___ deep - ly stuck in our ways. _ You _____

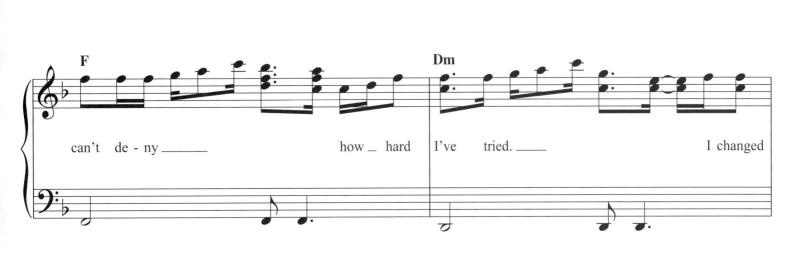

can't de - ny _____ how _ hard I've tried. _____ I changed

To Coda ⊕

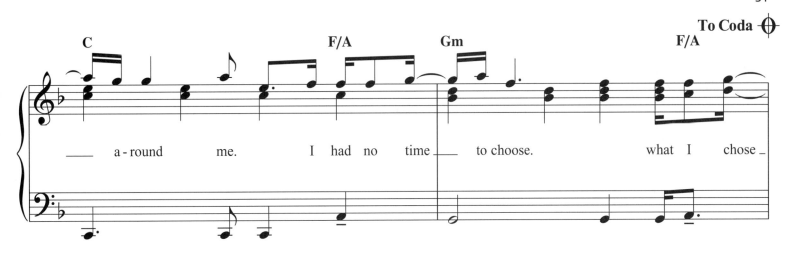

a - round me. I had no time ___ to choose. what I chose ___

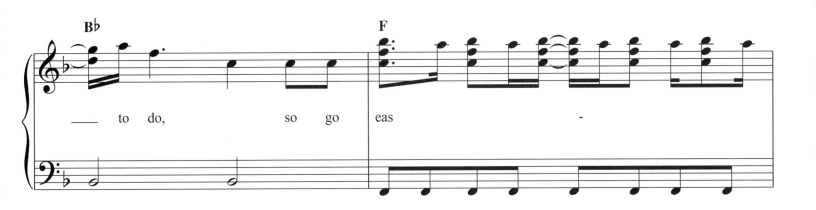

___ to do, so go eas

- y ___ on ___ me. ___

___ I had ___ good in - ten - tions ___

and the high - est hopes, but I know right now

it pro-b'ly does-n't e - ven show. Go

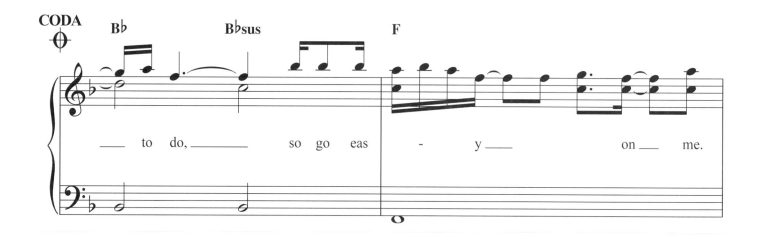

to do, so go eas - y on me.

THE FIRST TIME EVER I SAW YOUR FACE

Words and Music by
EWAN MacCOLL

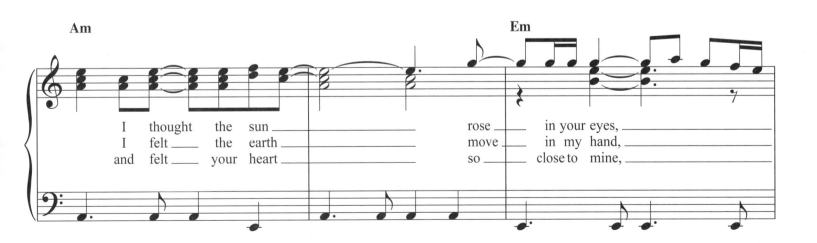

and the moon ___ and the stars ___
like the trem - bling heart ___
and I knew ___ our joy ___

were the gifts you gave ___ to
of a cap - tive bird ___ that
would fill the earth ___

___ the dark ___
___ was there ___

and the end of the skies.
at my com -

mand.

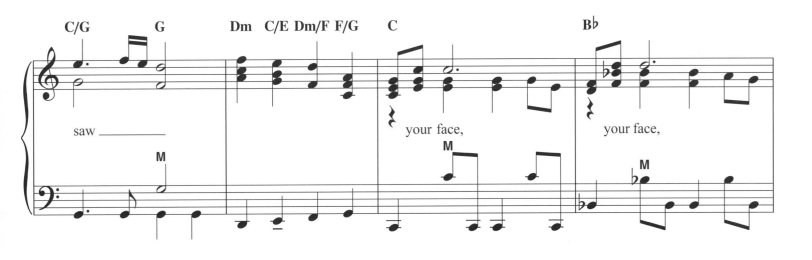

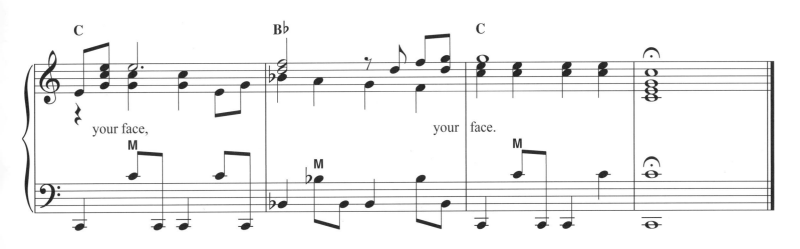

GABRIEL'S OBOE
from the Motion Picture THE MISSION

Music by
ENNIO MORRICONE

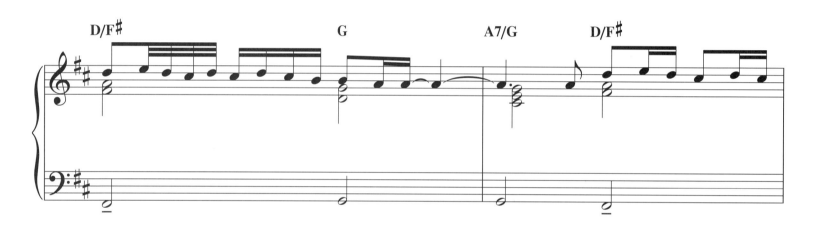

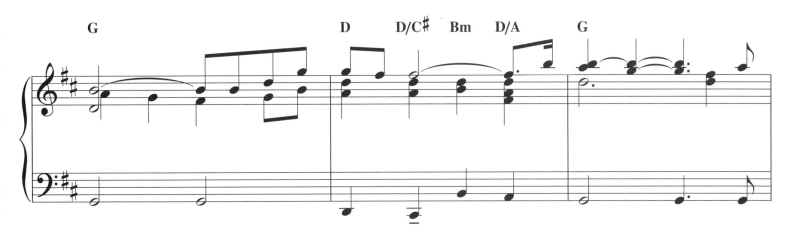

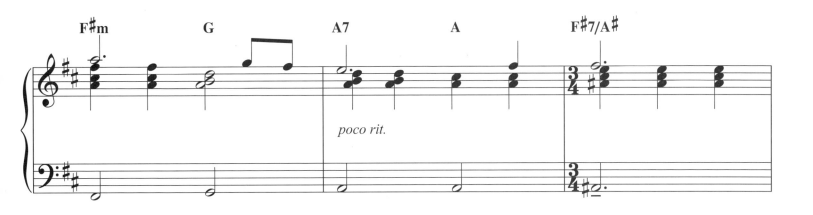

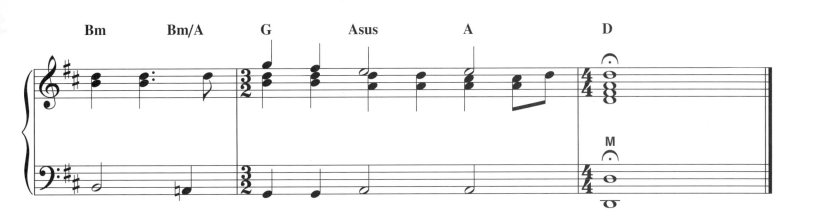

HOW DEEP IS YOUR LOVE

from the Motion Picture SATURDAY NIGHT FEVER

Words and Music by BARRY GIBB,
ROBIN GIBB and MAURICE GIBB

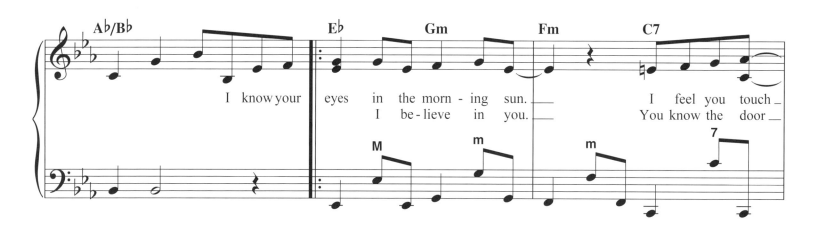

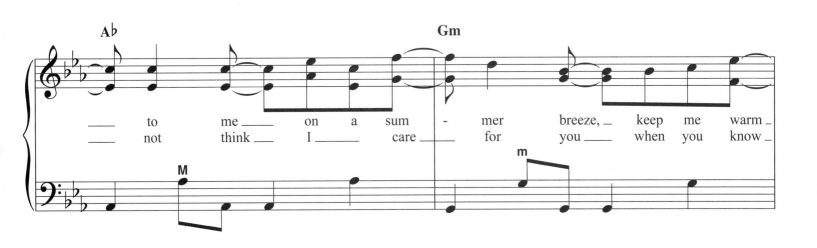

I real - ly mean ___ to learn. ___ 'Cause we're liv - ing in a world of fools, ___

___ break - ing us down ___ when they all ___ should let ___ us be. ___

___ We be - long ___ to you ___ and me.

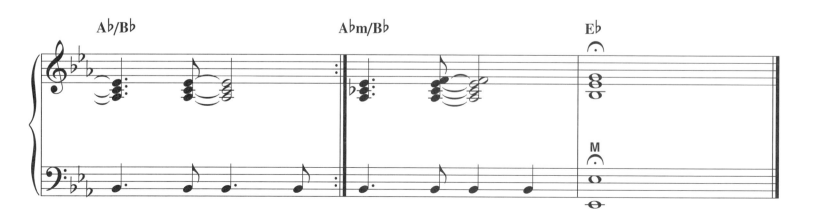

JAR OF HEARTS

Words and Music by BARRETT YERETSIAN,
CHRISTINA PERRI and DREW LAWRENCE

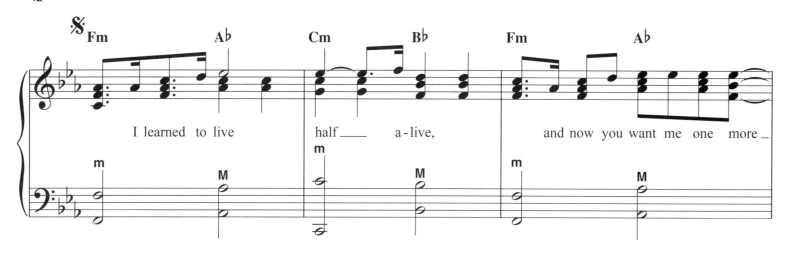

I learned to live half a-live, and now you want me one more

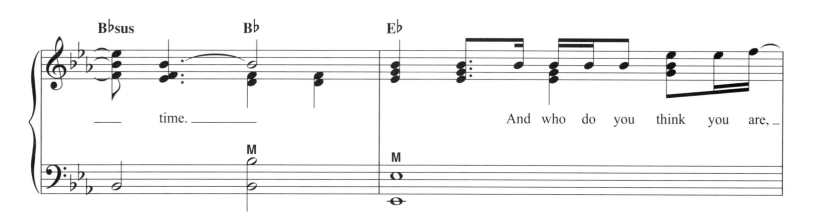

time. And who do you think you are,

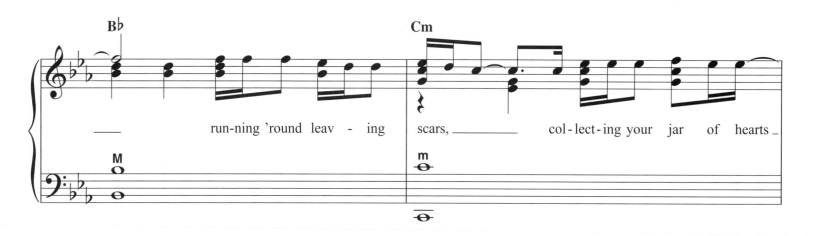

running 'round leav - ing scars, col-lect-ing your jar of hearts

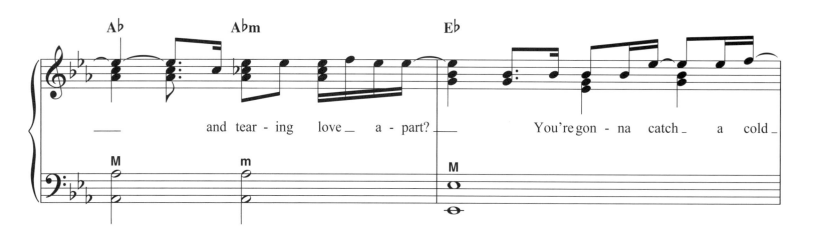

and tear - ing love a - part? You're gon - na catch a cold

from the ice in - side ___ your soul. _____ So don't come back for

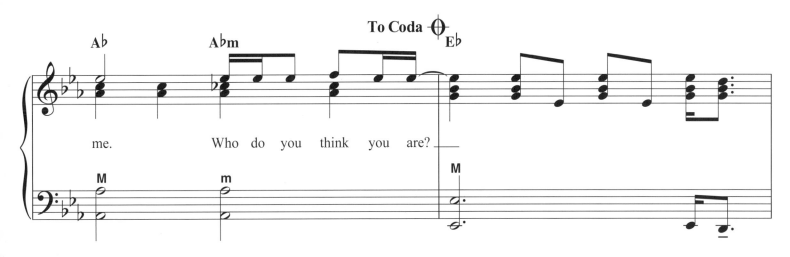

me. Who do you think you are? _____

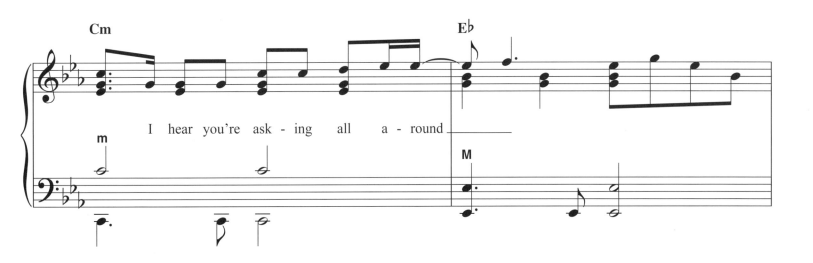

I hear you're ask - ing all a - round _____

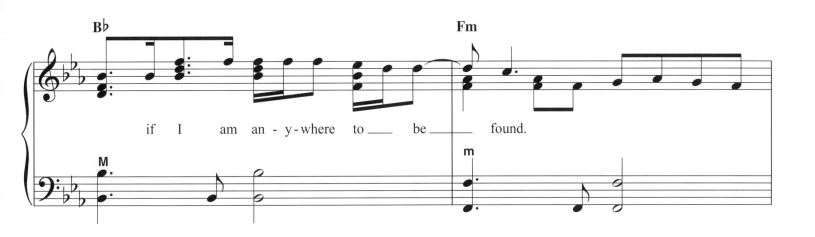

if I am an - y - where to ___ be _____ found.

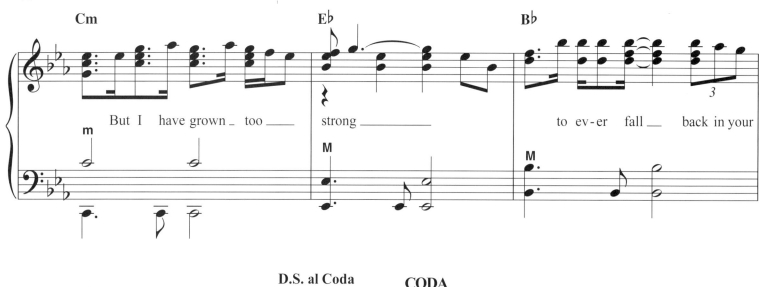

But I have grown _ too ____ strong _____ to ev-er fall ___ back in your

arms. _____

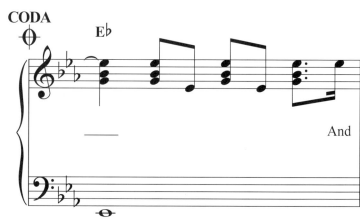

_____ And

it took so long just to feel al - right, _____ re-mem-ber ___ how to put back the

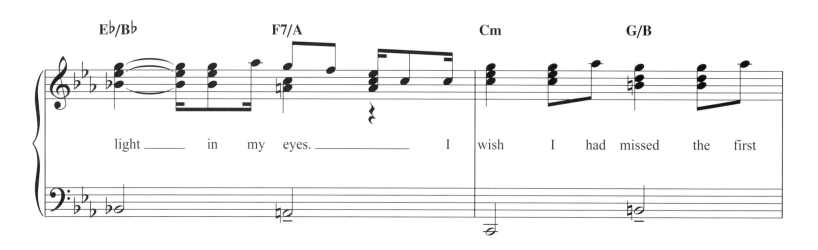

light _____ in my eyes. _____ I wish I had missed the first

time that we kissed _____ 'cause you broke all _____ your prom - is - es. And

now you're back, you don't get to get me back. _____

_____ And who do you think you are, _____ run-ning 'round leav - ing

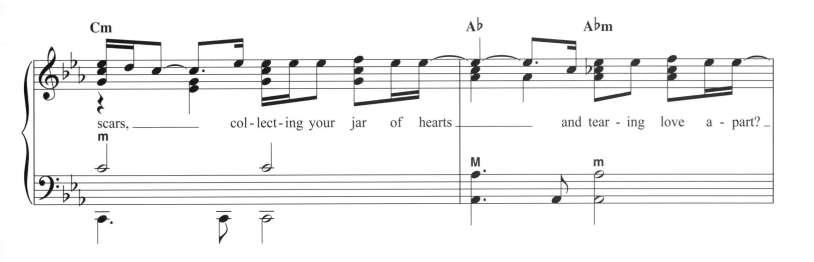

scars, _____ col - lect-ing your jar of hearts _____ and tear - ing love a - part? _____

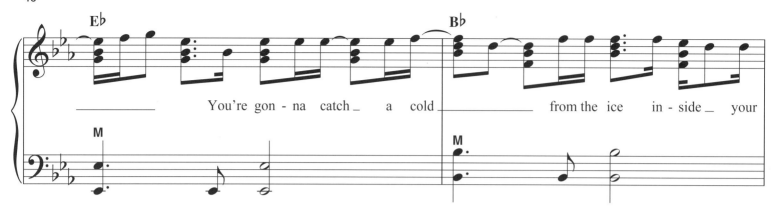

You're gon - na catch __ a cold __ from the ice in - side __ your

soul. __ So don't come back for me, don't come back __ at

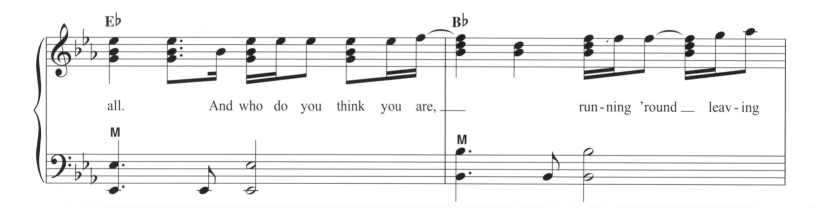

all. And who do you think you are, __ run - ning 'round __ leav - ing

scars, __ col - lect - ing your jar of hearts, __ tear - ing love a - part?

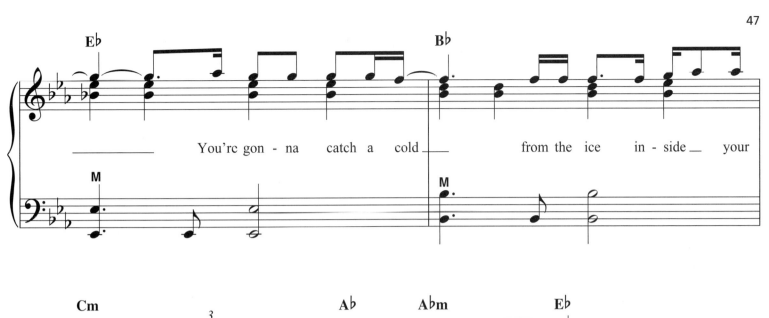

You're gon - na catch a cold _____ from the ice in - side _____ your

soul. _____ Don't come back _ for me, don't come back at all.

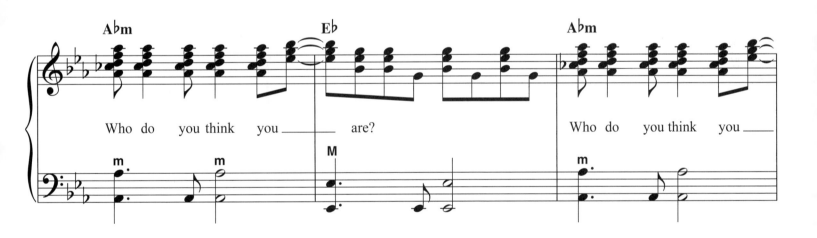

Who do you think you _____ are? Who do you think you _____

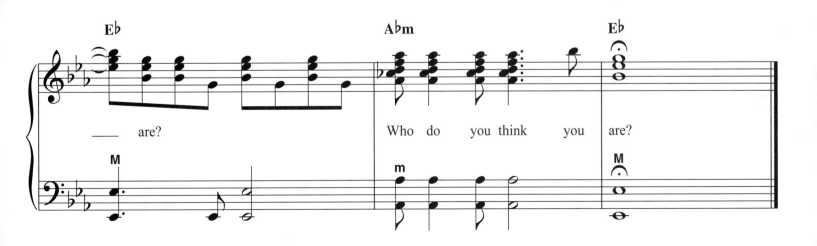

_____ are? Who do you think you are?

KILLING ME SOFTLY WITH HIS SONG

Words by NORMAN GIMBEL
Music by CHARLES FOX

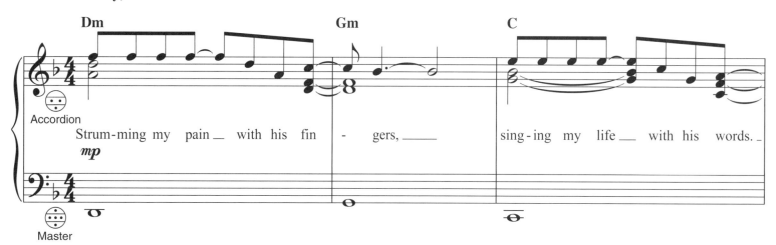

words, kill - ing me soft - ly _____ with his song. _

I heard he sang _____ a good _ song,
I felt all flushed with fe - ver,
He sang as if _____ he knew me

I heard he had _
em - bar - rassed by
in all my dark

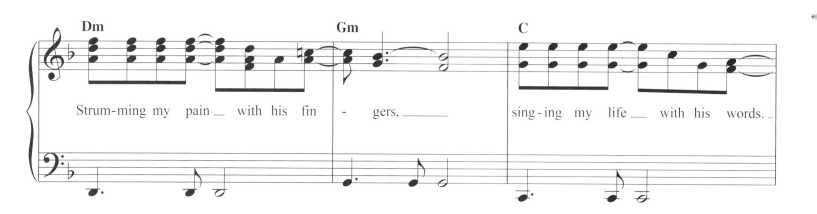

Kill - ing me soft - ly with his ___ song, kill - ing me soft -

- ly ___ with his ___ song, tell - ing my whole ___ life ___ with his ___

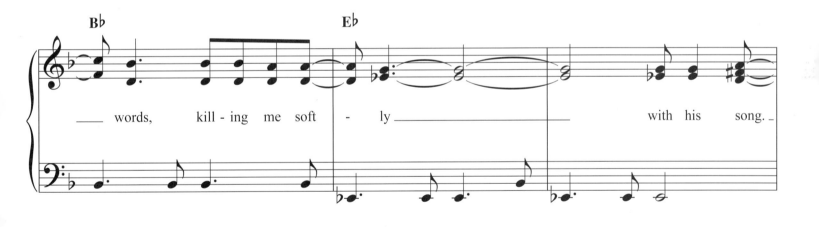

___ words, kill - ing me soft - ly ___ with his song. ___

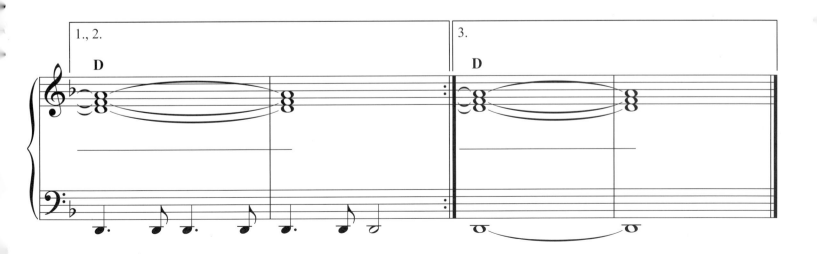

LADY

Words and Music by
LIONEL RICHIE

Moderately slow, with feeling

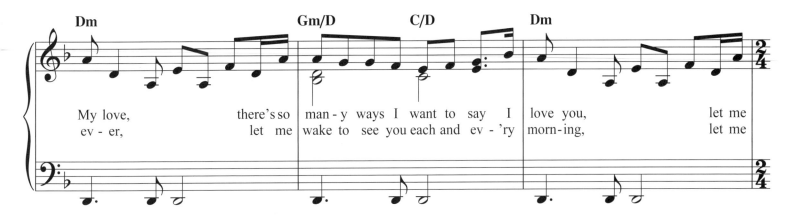

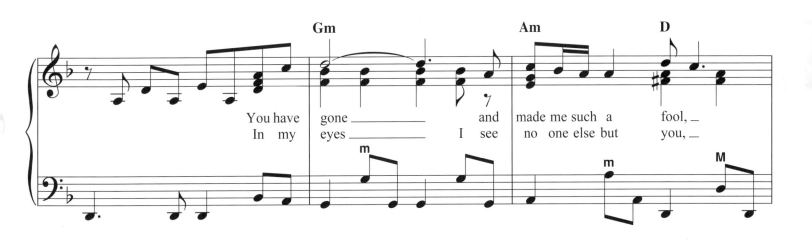

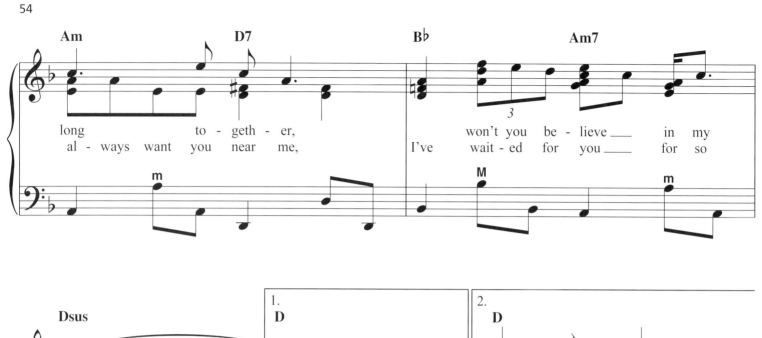

long   to - geth - er,   won't you be - lieve ___ in my
al - ways want you near me,   I've wait - ed for you ___ for so

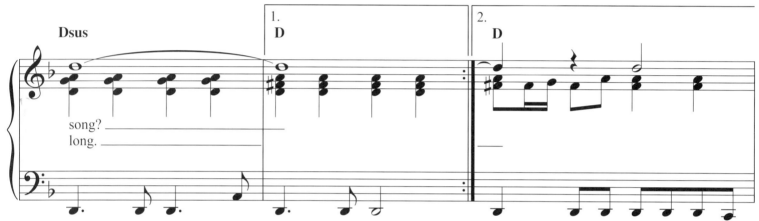

song? ___
long. ___

La - dy, _____   your   loves's   the   on - ly love I need,

and be - side   me   is   where

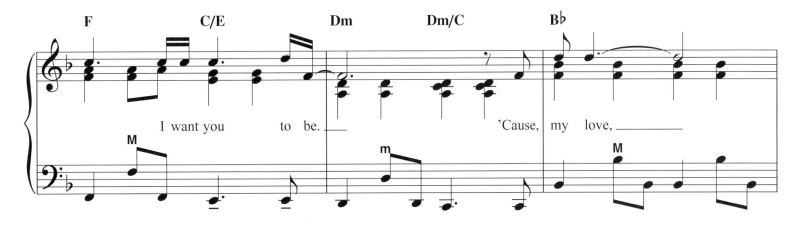

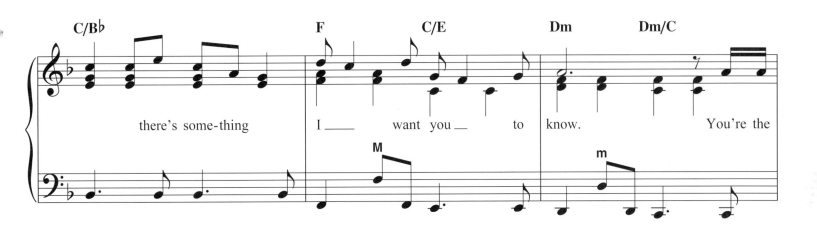

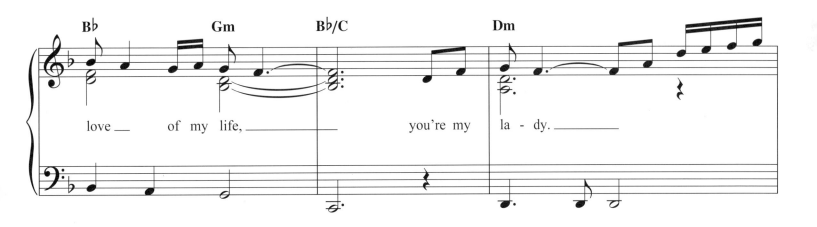

THE LONG AND WINDING ROAD

Words and Music by JOHN LENNON
and PAUL McCARTNEY

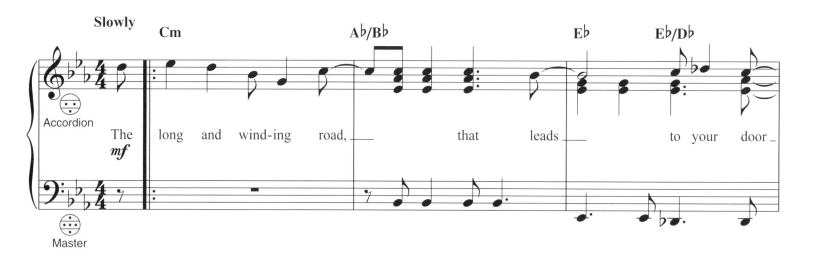

The long and wind-ing road, ___ that leads ___ to your door ___

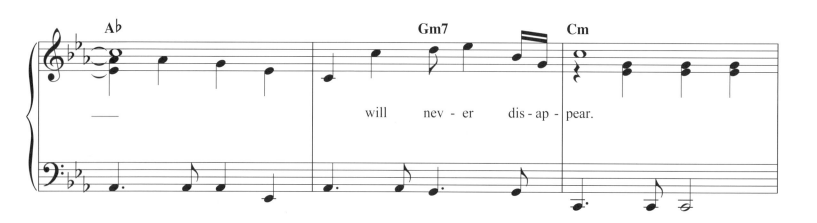

___ will nev - er dis - ap - pear.

I've seen that road be - fore. ___

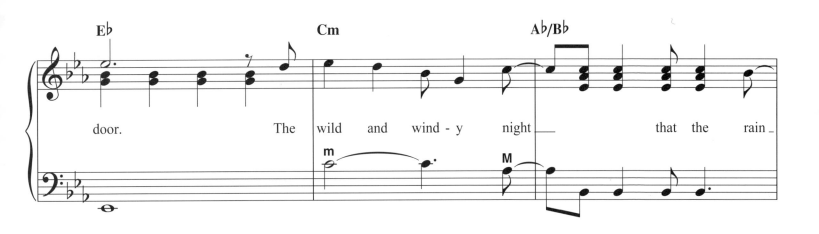

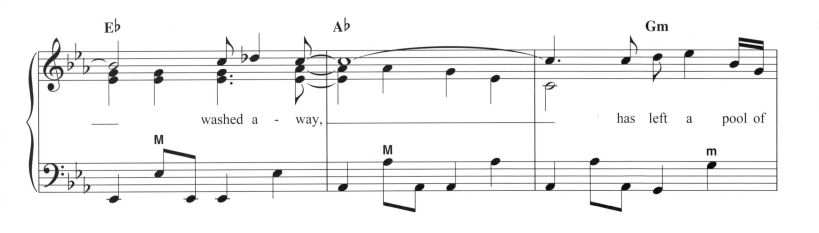

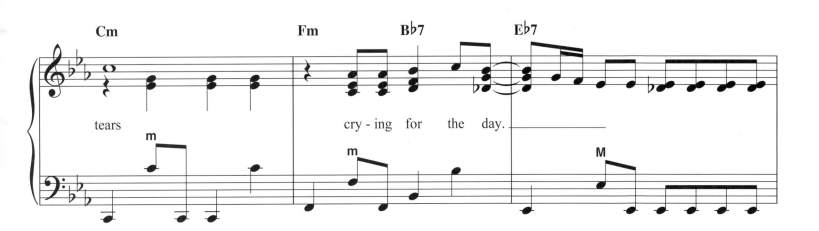

Why leave me stand-ing here? Let me know the way.

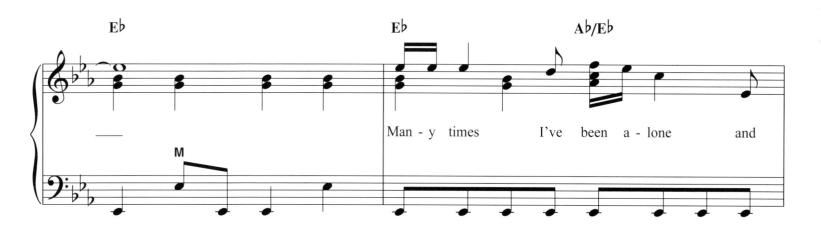

Man - y times I've been a - lone and

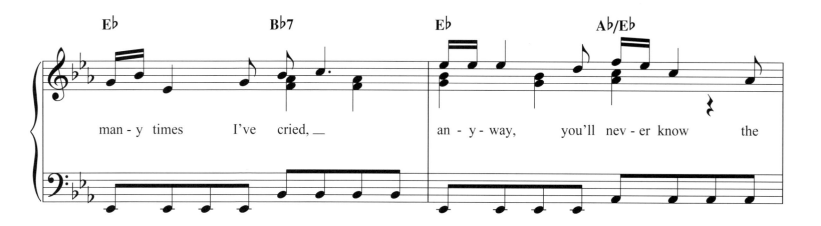

man - y times I've cried, __ an - y - way, you'll nev - er know the

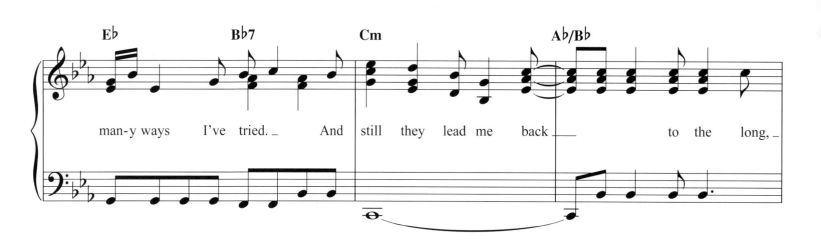

man - y ways I've tried. __ And still they lead me back __ to the long, __

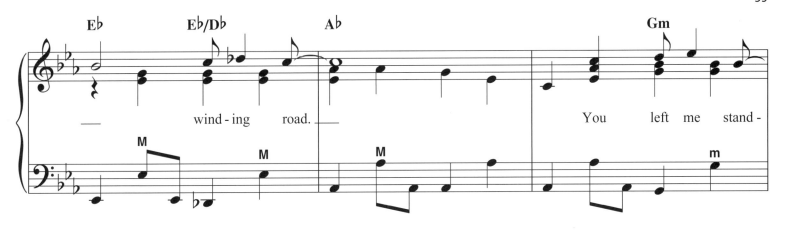

wind - ing   road.   You   left   me   stand -

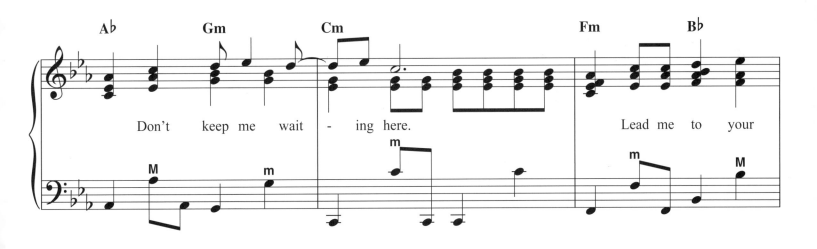

- ing here   a long, long time   a - go.

Don't   keep   me   wait - ing here.   Lead   me   to   your

door.

PERFECT

Words and Music by
ED SHEERAN

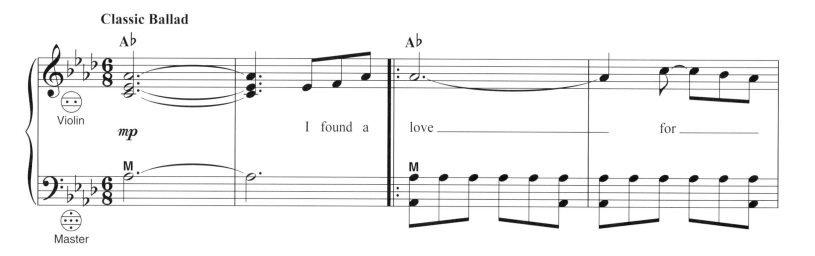

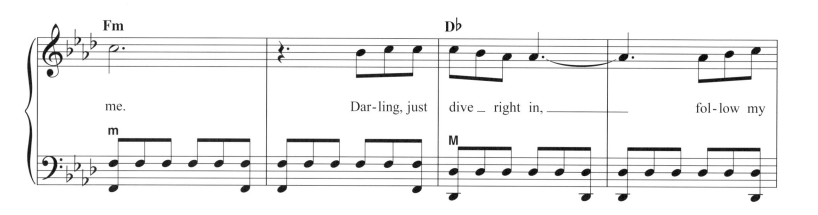

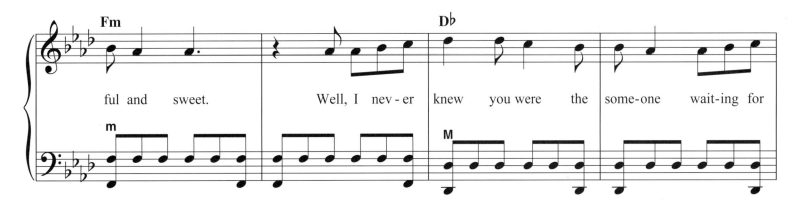

ful and sweet. Well, I nev - er knew you were the some-one wait-ing for

me. _____ 'Cause we were just kids when we {fell in / so in

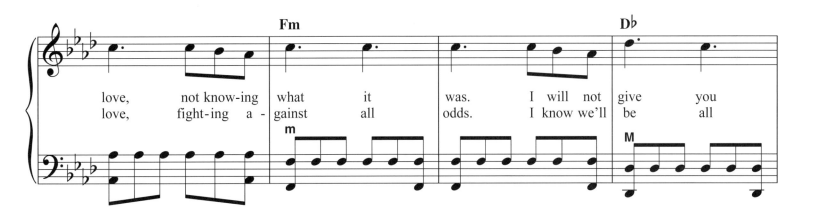

love, not know-ing what it was. I will not give you
love, fight-ing a - gainst it all odds. I know we'll be all

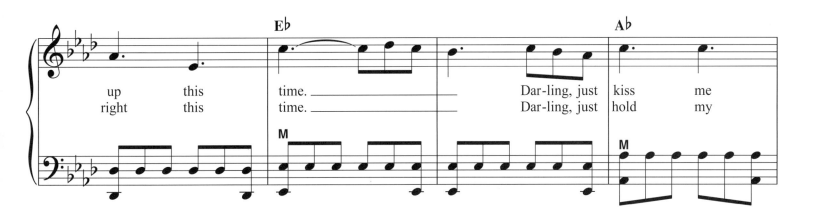

up this time. _____ Dar-ling, just kiss me
right this time. _____ Dar-ling, just hold my

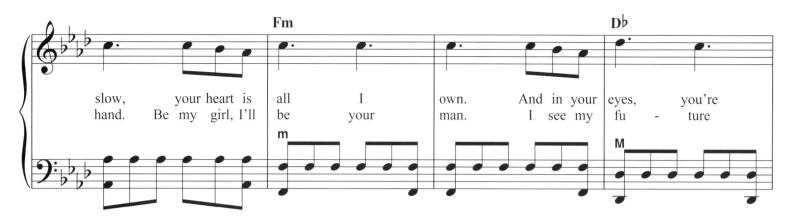

slow,   your heart is   all   I   own.   And in your   eyes,   you're
hand.   Be my girl, I'll   be   your   man.   I   see my   fu - ture

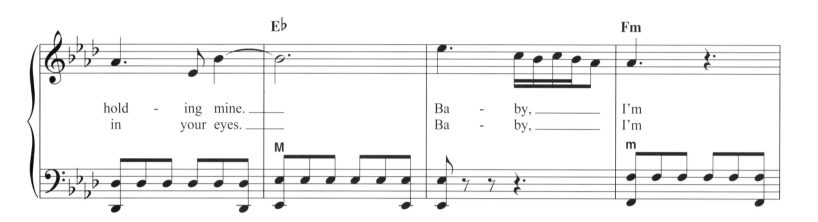

hold - ing mine. _____   Ba - by, _____   I'm
in   your eyes. _____   Ba - by, _____   I'm

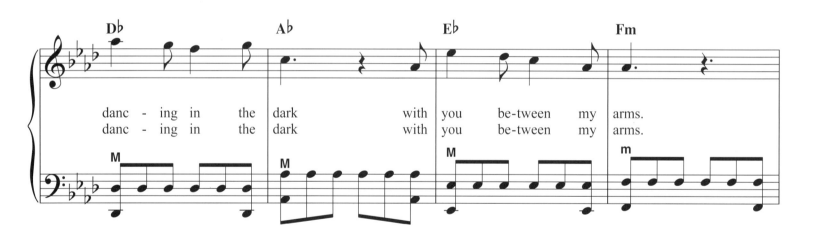

danc - ing in   the dark   with you   be-tween   my   arms.
danc - ing in   the dark   with you   be-tween   my   arms.

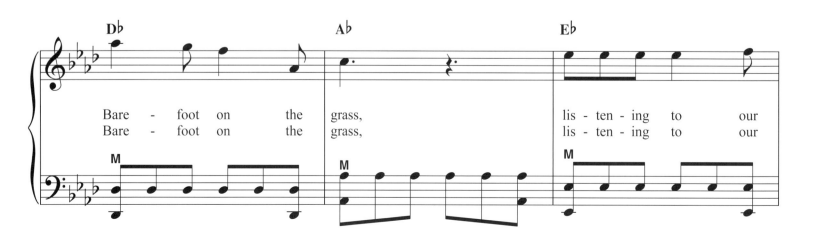

Bare - foot on   the   grass,   lis - ten-ing to   our
Bare - foot on   the   grass,   lis - ten-ing to   our

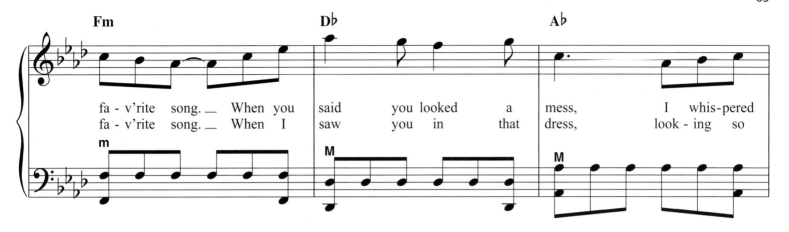

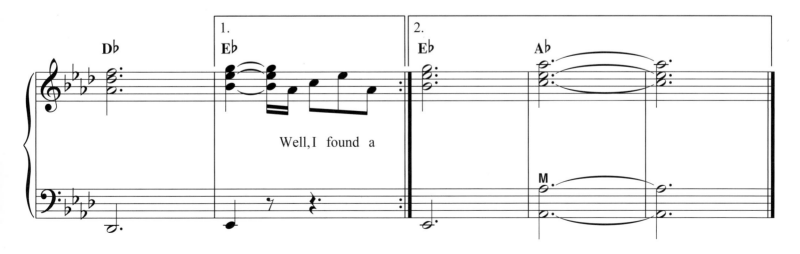

PIANO MAN

Words and Music by
BILLY JOEL

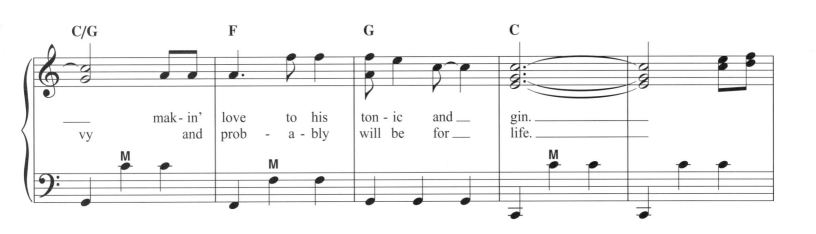

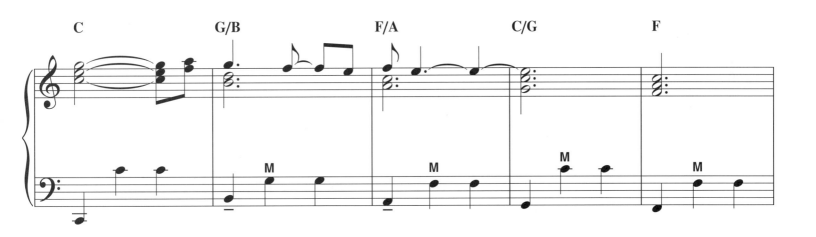

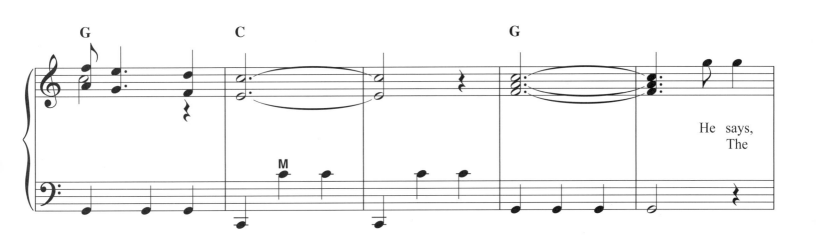

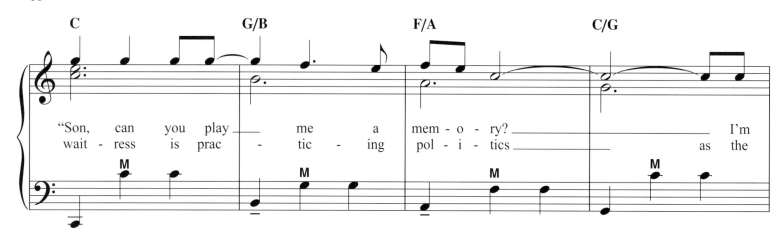

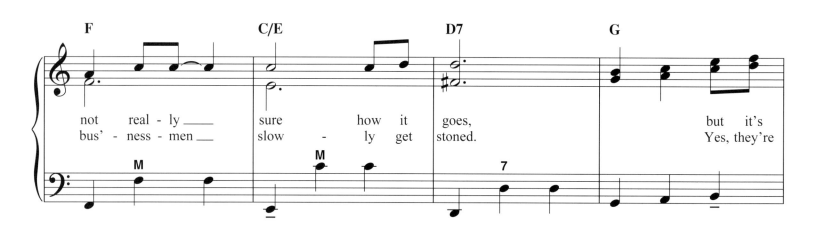

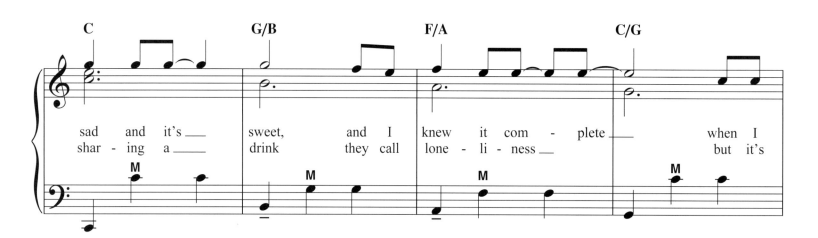

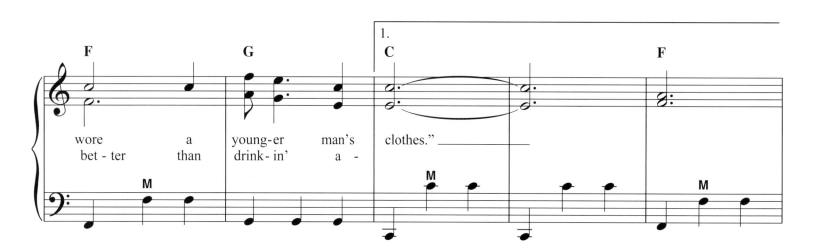

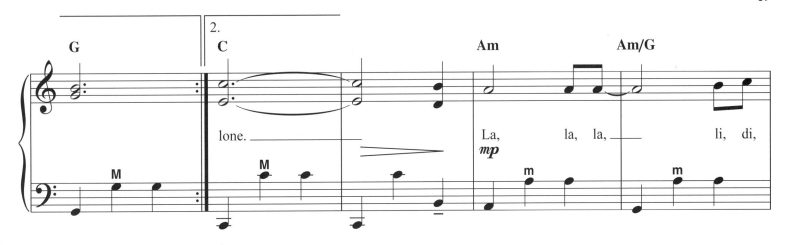

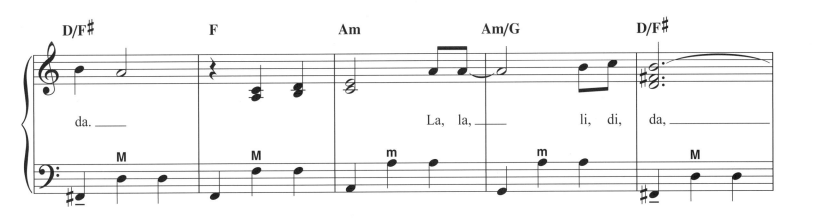

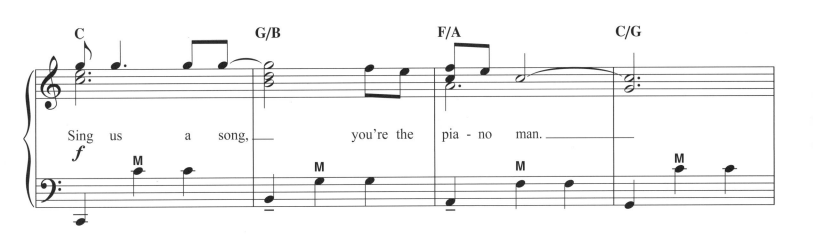

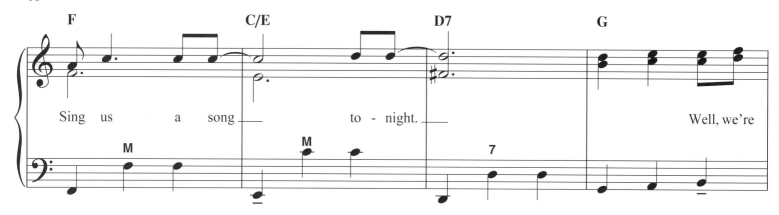

Sing us a song _____ to - night. _____ Well, we're

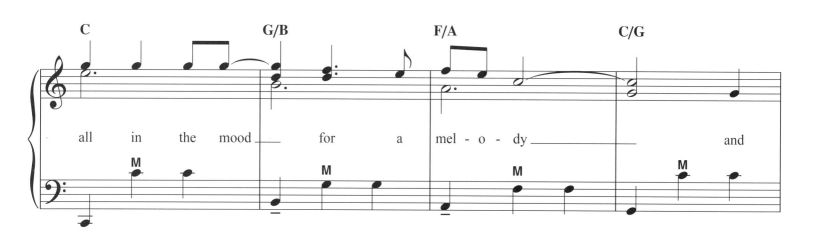

all in the mood _____ for a mel - o - dy _____ and

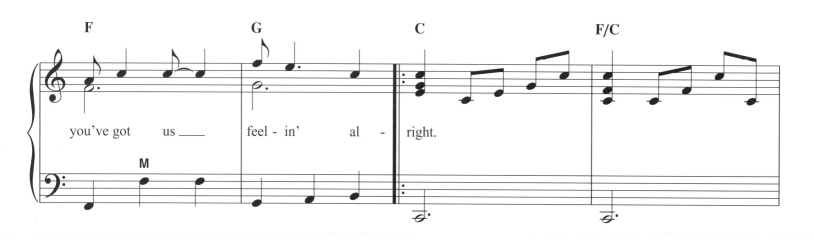

you've got us _____ feel - in' al - right.

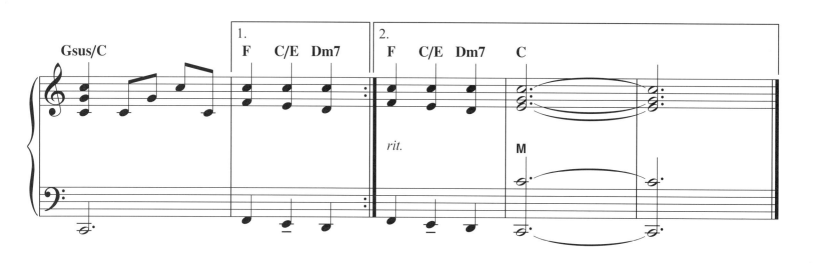

THE RAINBOW CONNECTION

from THE MUPPET MOVIE

Words and Music by PAUL WILLIAMS
and KENNETH L. ASCHER

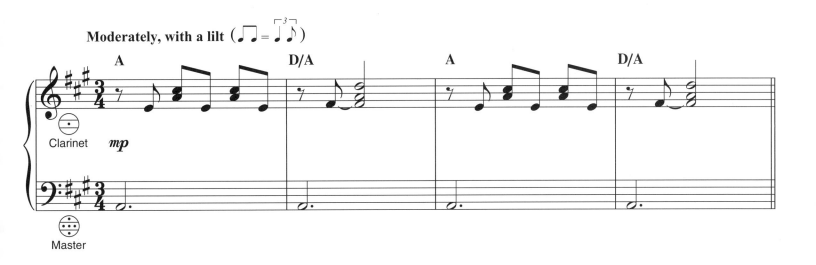

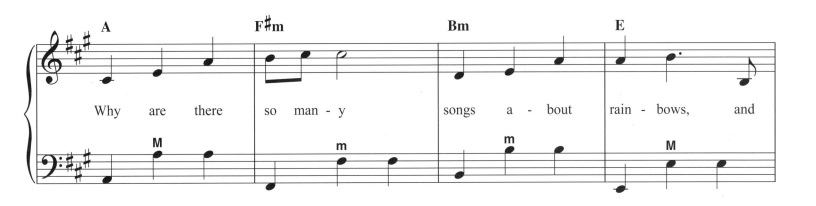

Why are there so man-y songs a - bout rain - bows, and

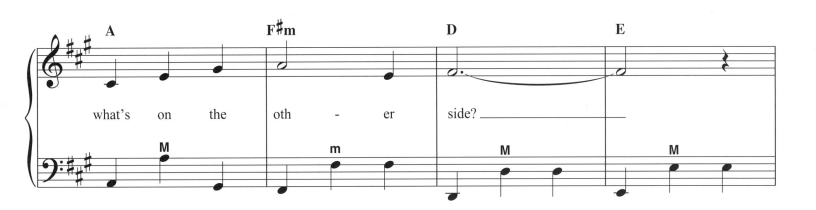

what's on the oth - er side?

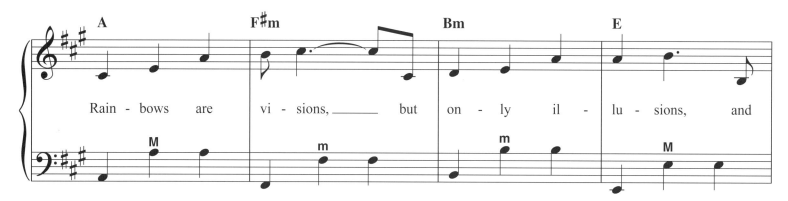

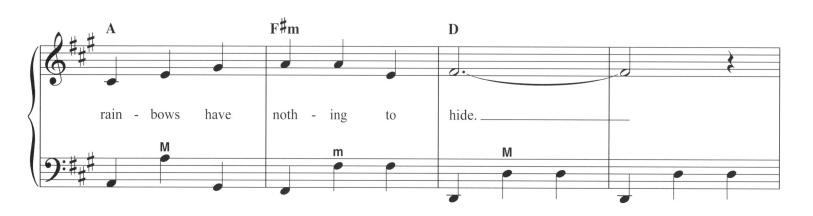

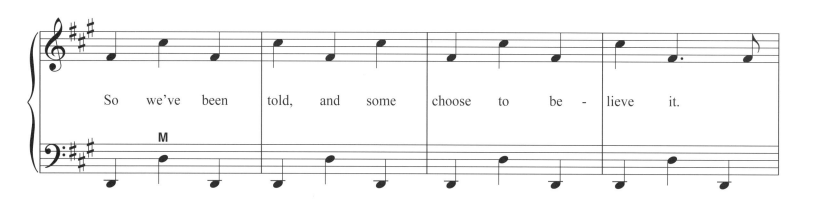

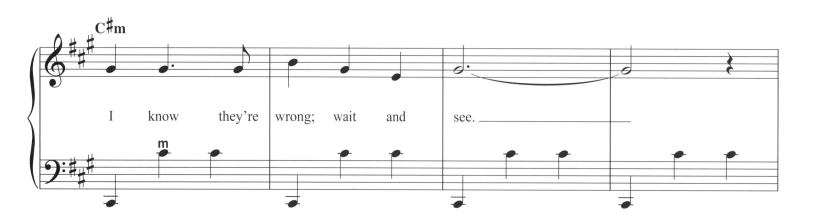

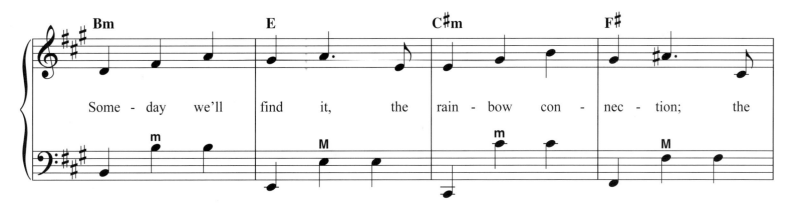

Some - day we'll find it, the rain - bow con - nec - tion; the

lov - ers, the dream-ers and me.

Who said that ev - 'ry wish would

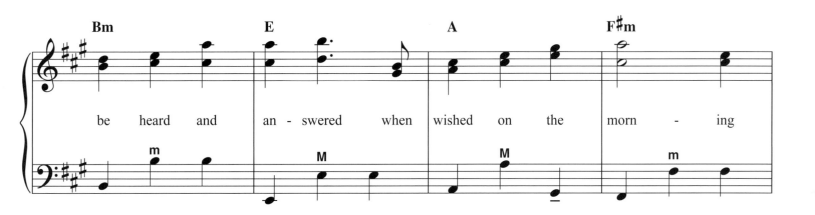

be heard and an - swered when wished on the morn - ing

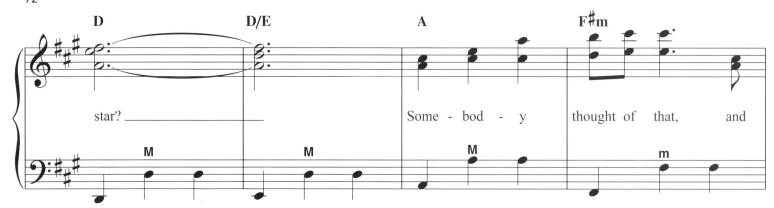

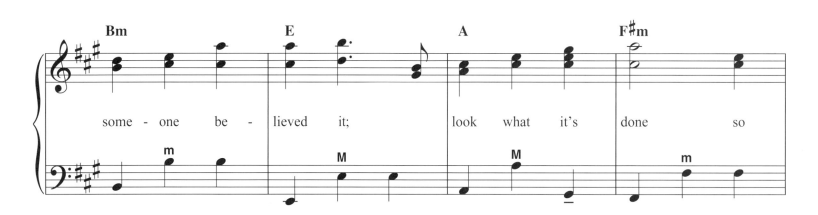

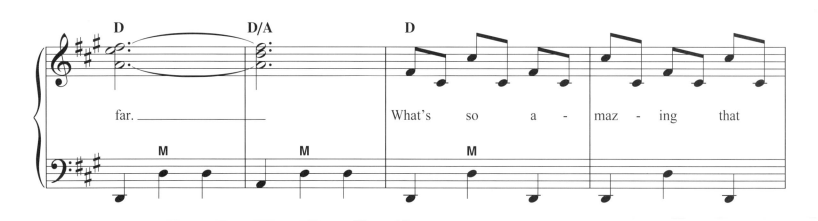

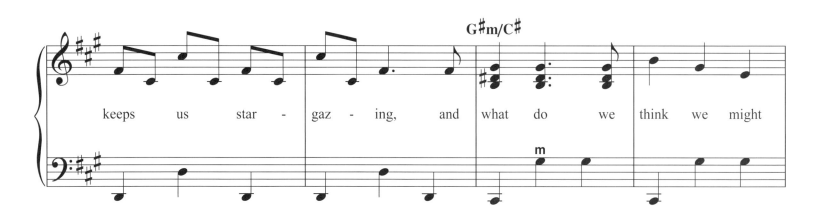

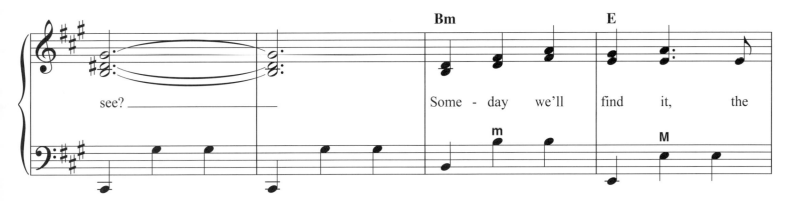

see? _____ Some - day we'll find it, the

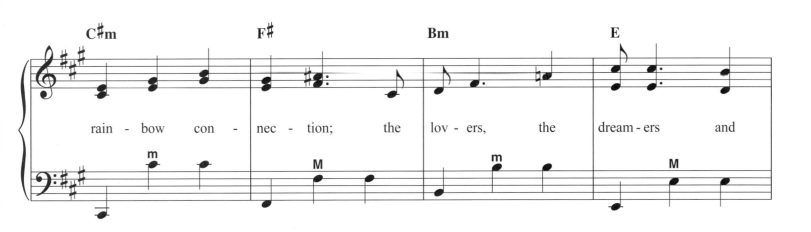

rain - bow con - nec - tion; the lov - ers, the dream - ers and

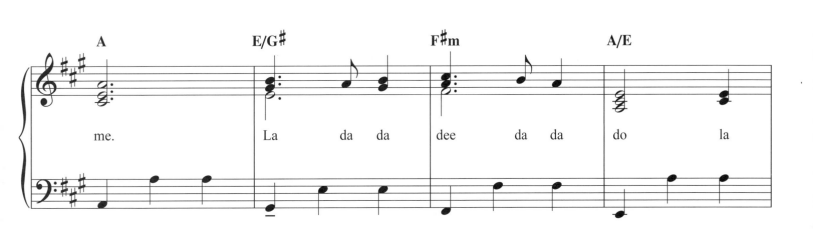

me. La da da dee da da do la

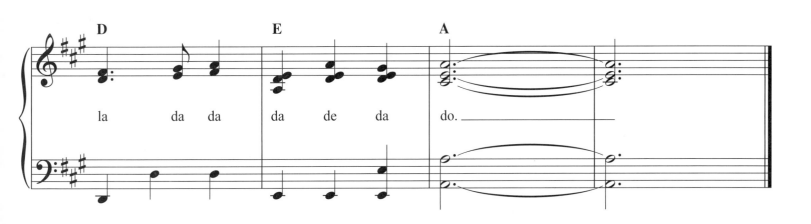

la da da da de da do. _____

THE ROSE

from the Twentieth Century-Fox Motion Picture Release THE ROSE

Words and Music by
AMANDA McBROOM

flow - er, _____ and you, _____ its on - ly seed.

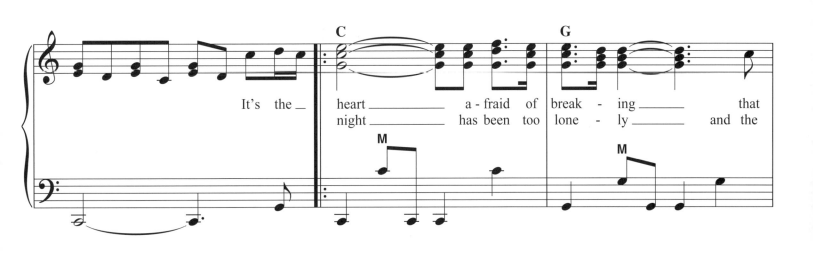

It's the _ heart _____ a - fraid of break - ing _____ that
night _____ has been too lone - ly _____ and the

nev - er _____ learns to _ dance. It's the _ dream _____ a - fraid of
road _____ has been too _ long, and you _ think _____ that love is

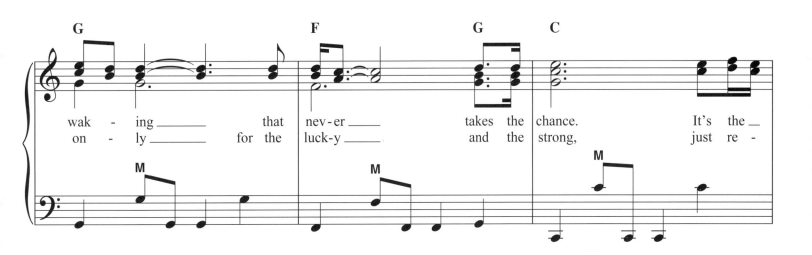

wak - ing _____ that nev - er _____ takes the chance. It's the _
on - ly _____ for the luck - y _____ and the strong, just re -

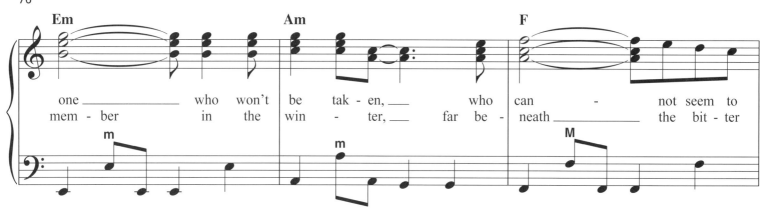

one _____ who won't be tak - en, ___ who can - not seem to
mem - ber in the win - ter, ___ far be - neath _____ the bit - ter

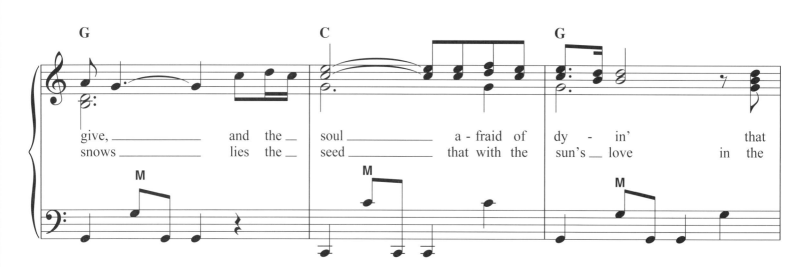

give, _____ and the __ soul _____ a - fraid of dy - in' that
snows _____ lies the __ seed _____ that with the sun's __ love in the

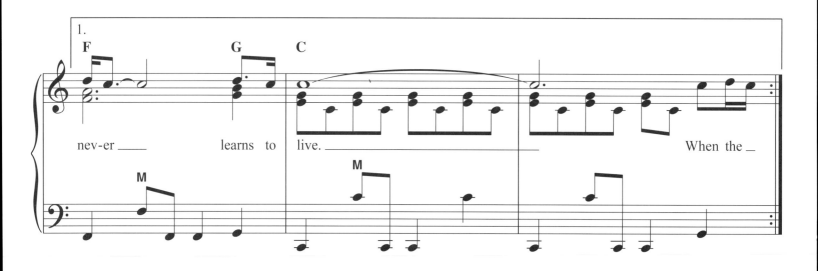

nev-er ____ learns to live. _____ When the __

spring _____ be-comes the rose.

WHEN I WAS YOUR MAN

Words and Music by BRUNO MARS,
ARI LEVINE, PHILIP LAWRENCE
and ANDREW WYATT

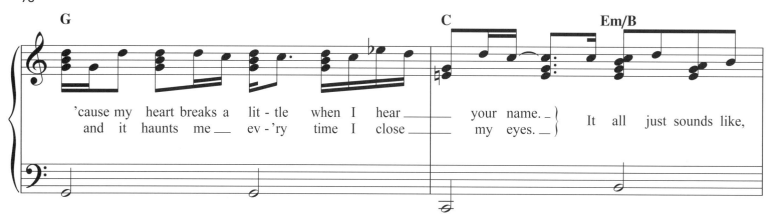

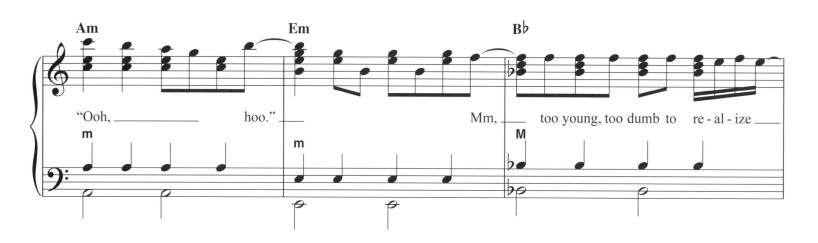

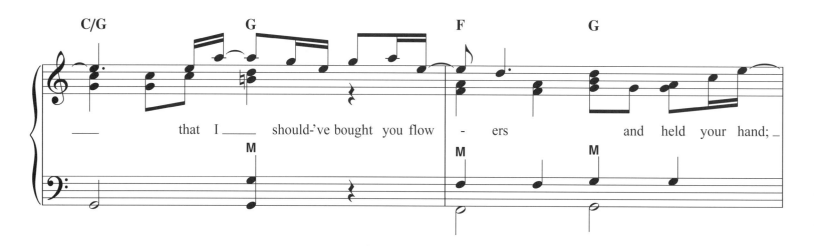

SAY SOMETHING

Words and Music by IAN AXEL,
CHAD VACCARINO and MIKE CAMPBELL

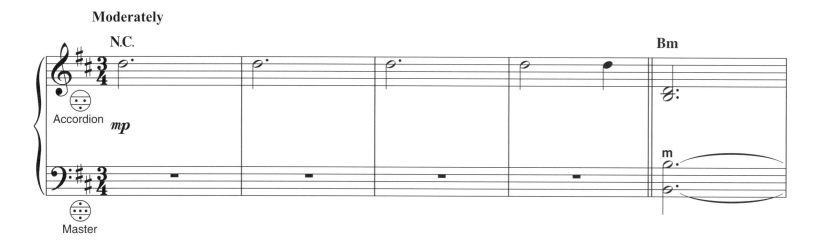

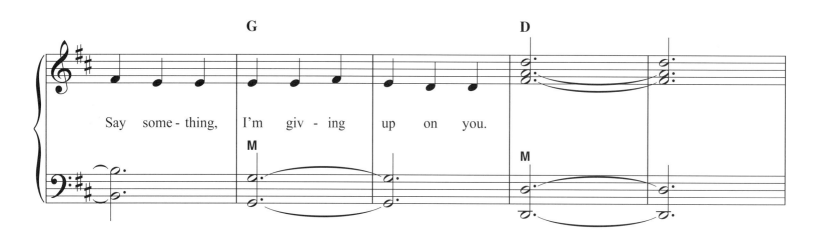

Say some-thing, I'm giv-ing up on you.

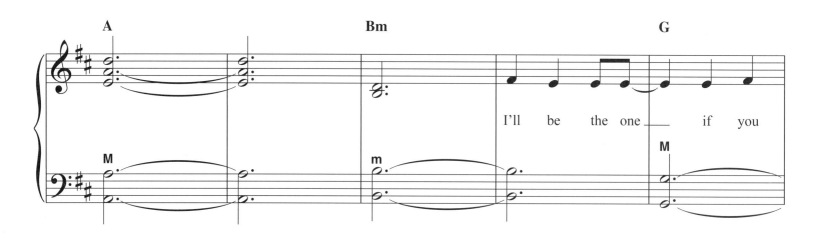

I'll be the one___ if you

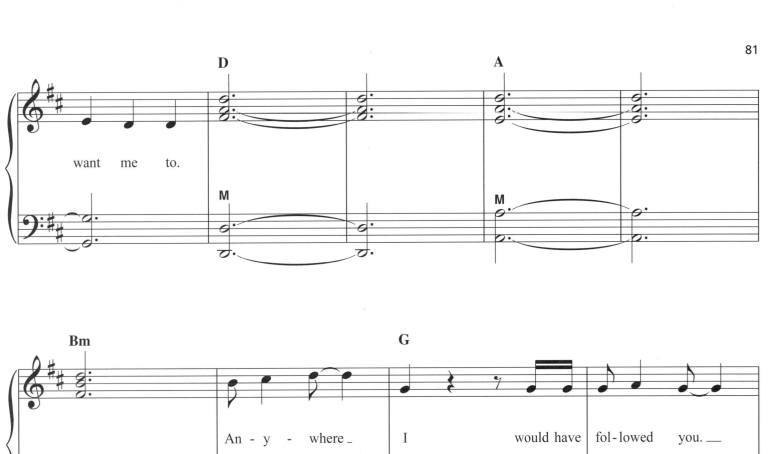

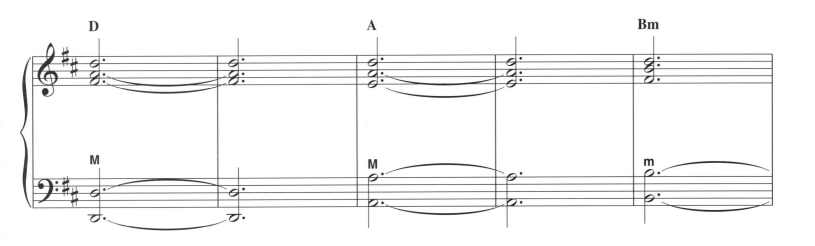

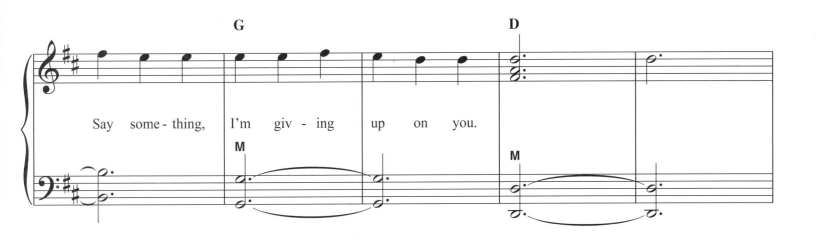

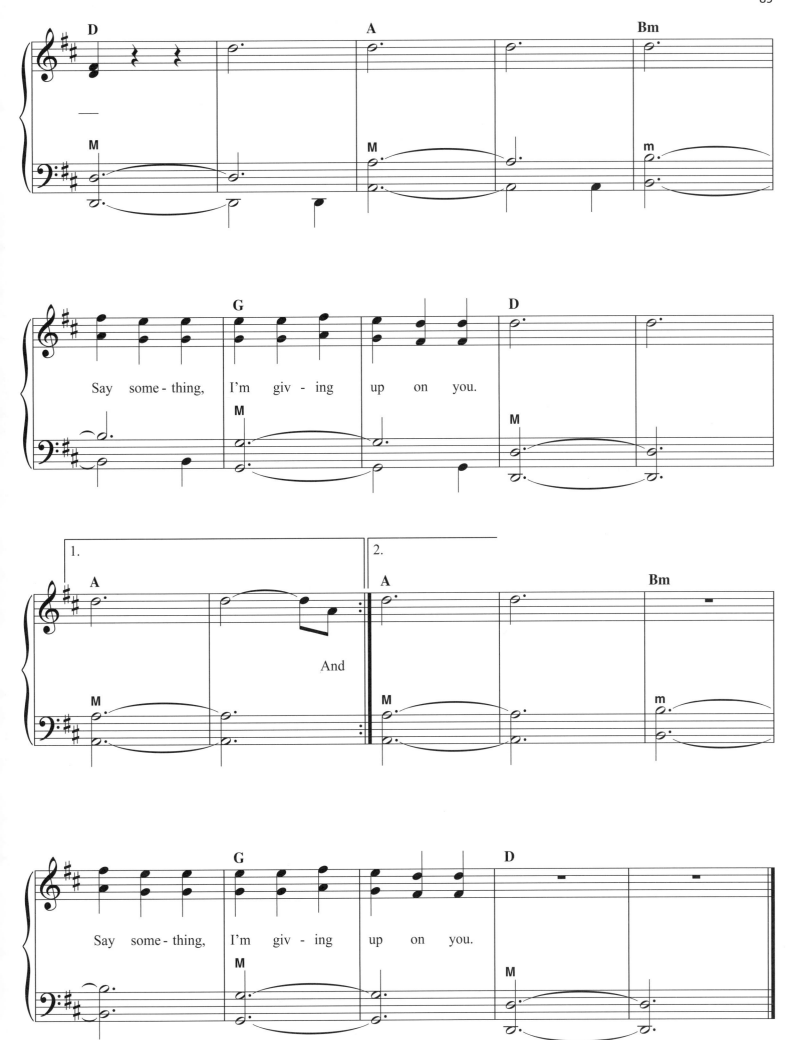

THE SOUND OF SILENCE

Words and Music by
PAUL SIMON

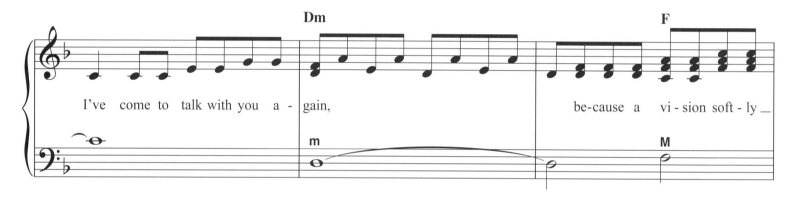

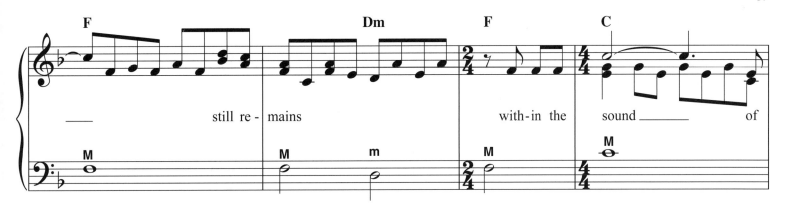

still re - mains   with-in the   sound _____ of

si - lence.   *mp* In rest-less dreams I walked a - lone
                                   And in the na - ked light I saw

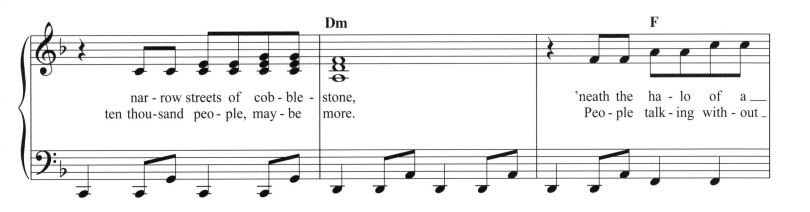

nar - row streets of cob - ble - stone,   'neath the ha - lo of a ___
ten thou-sand peo - ple, may - be more.   Peo - ple talk - ing with - out ___

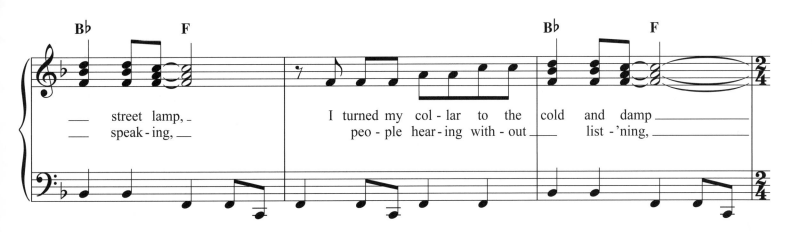

___ street lamp, ___   I turned my col - lar to the cold and damp _____
___ speak - ing, ___   peo - ple hear-ing with - out ___ list - 'ning, _____

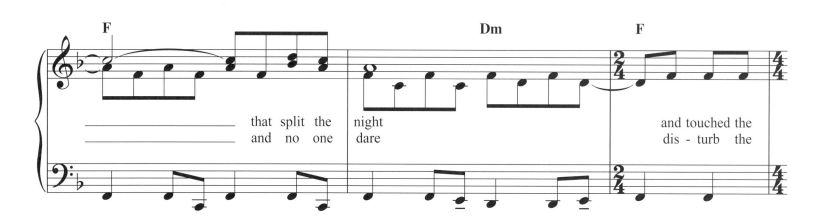

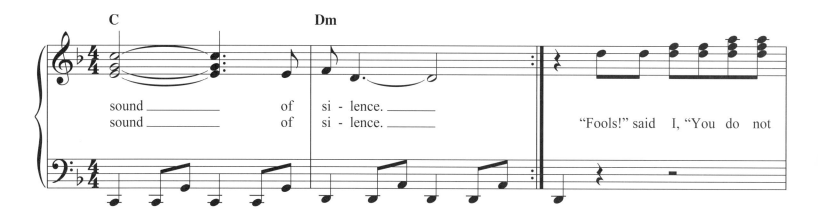

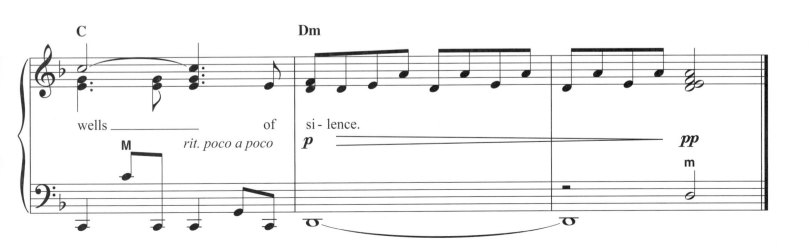

STAY WITH ME

Words and Music by SAM SMITH,
JAMES NAPIER, WILLIAM EDWARD PHILLIPS,
TOM PETTY and JEFF LYNNE

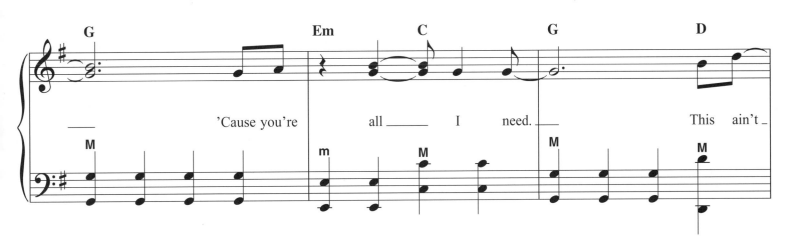

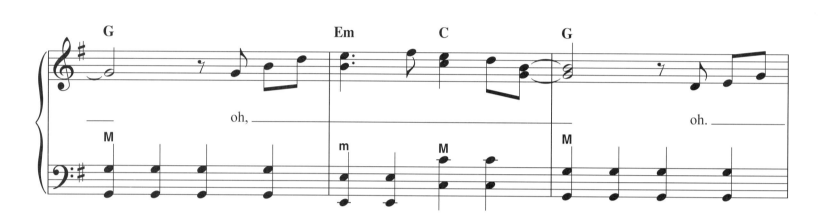

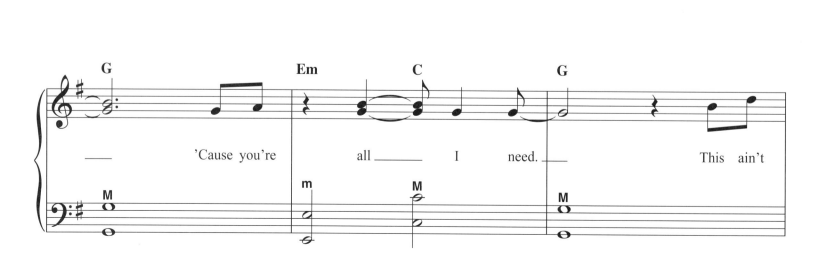

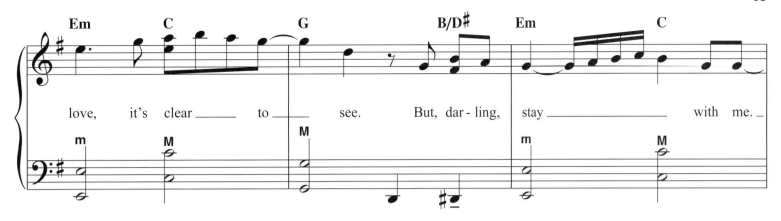

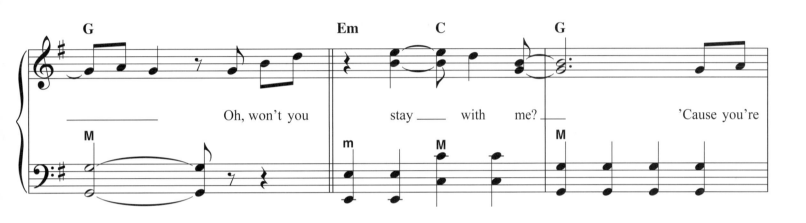

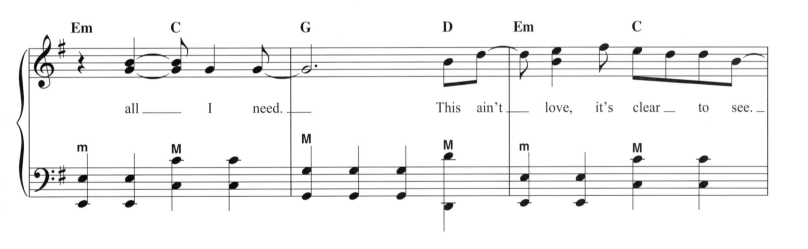

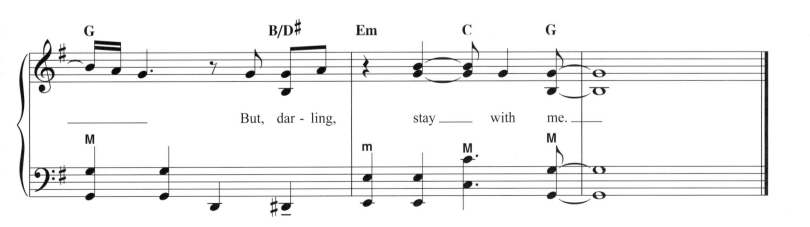

TIME IN A BOTTLE

Words and Music by
JIM CROCE

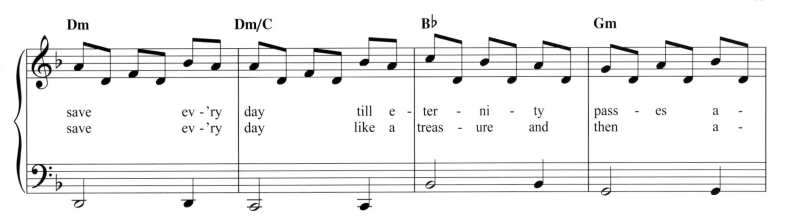

save ev -'ry day till e - ter - ni - ty pass - es a -
save ev -'ry day like a treas - ure and then a -

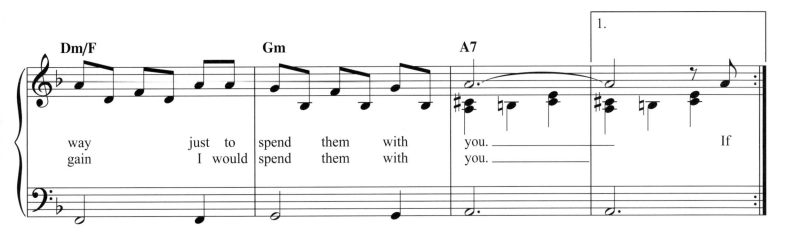

1.

way just to spend them with you. _____ If
gain I would spend them with you. _____

2. %

But there nev - er seems to be e -nough time ___ to do the things you

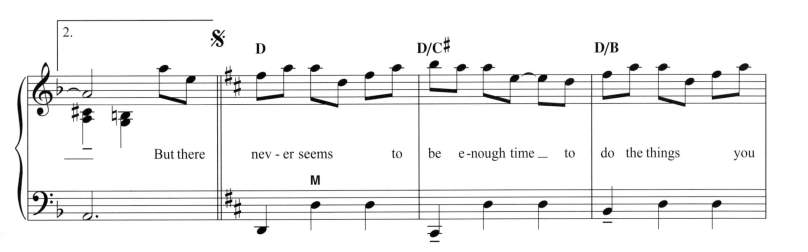

want to do once you find them.

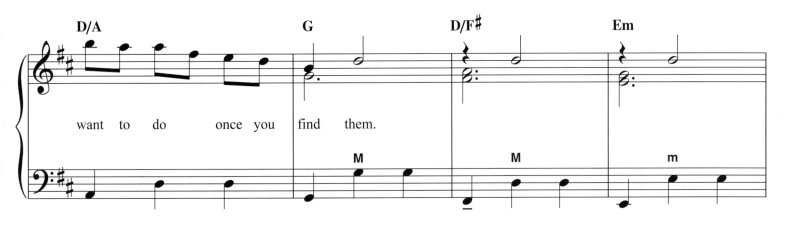

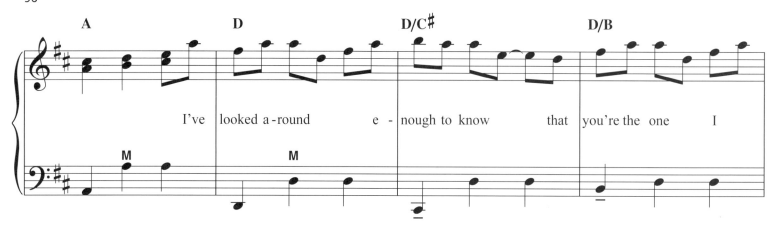

I've looked a-round e - nough to know that you're the one I

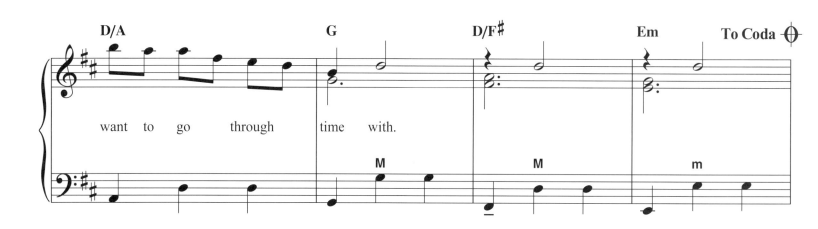

want to go through time with.

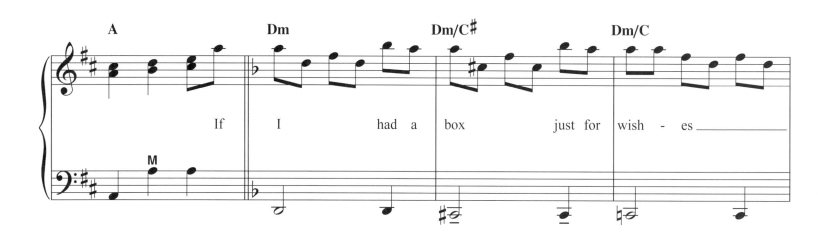

If I had a box just for wish - es

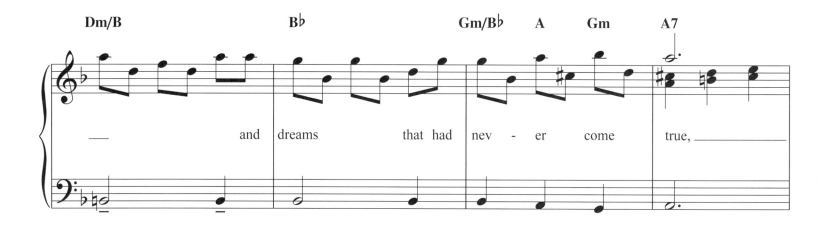

and dreams that had nev - er come true,

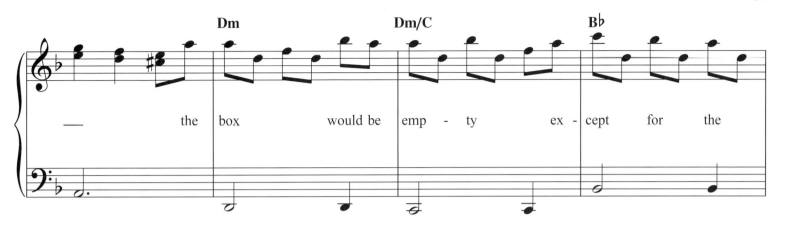

the box   would be   emp - ty   ex - cept   for   the

mem - 'ry   of   how   they were   an - swered   by   you. _____

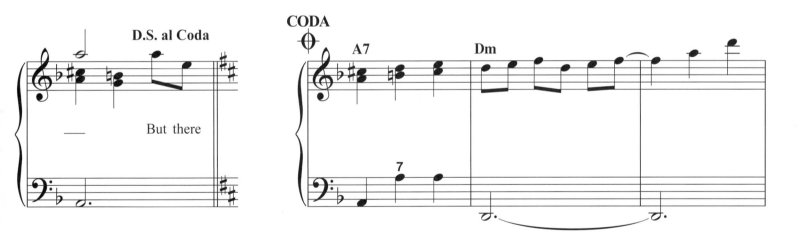

D.S. al Coda   **CODA**

_____   But there   A7   Dm

YOU ARE THE SUNSHINE OF MY LIFE

Words and Music by
STEVIE WONDER

Moderately, with feeling

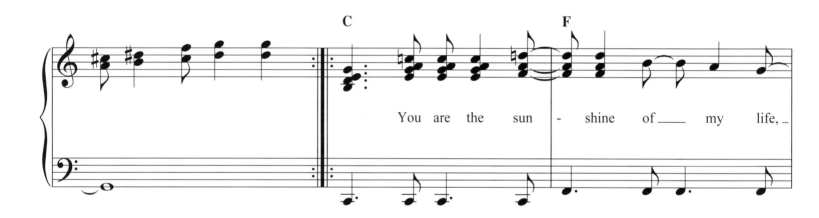

You are the sun - shine of ___ my life, ___

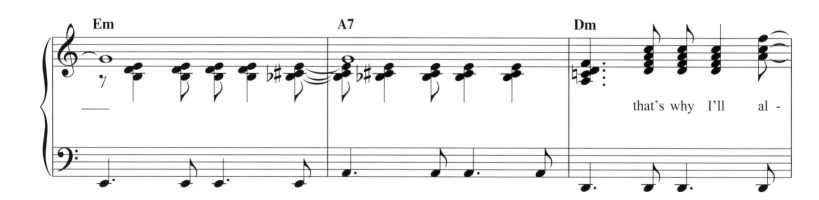

that's why I'll al-

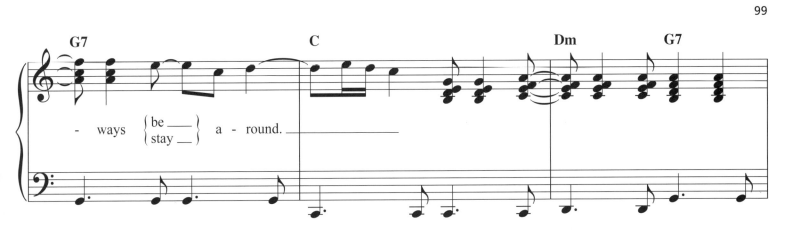

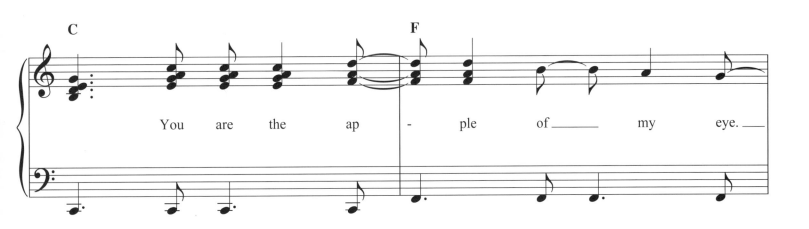

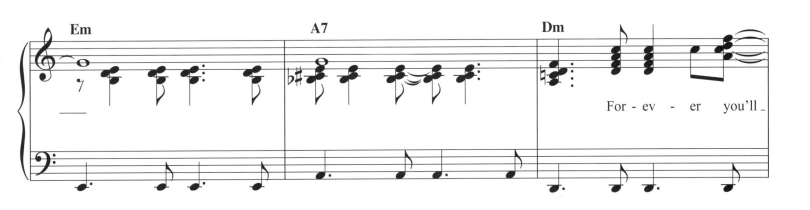

I feel like this ____ is the ____ be -
You must have known ____ is that I ____ was

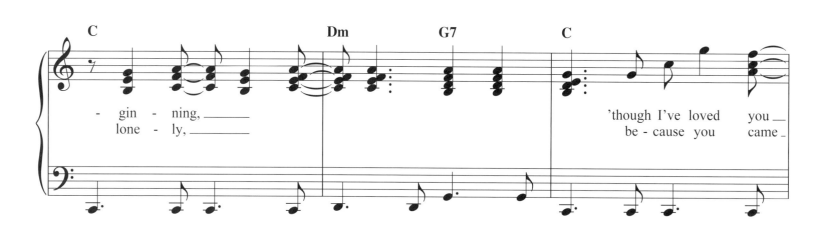

- gin - ning, ____
lone - ly, ____

'though I've loved you ____
be - cause you came _

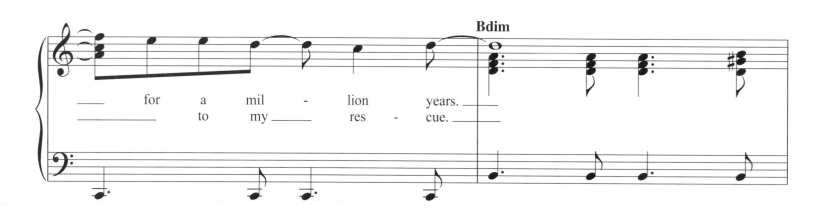

____ for a mil - lion years. ____
____ to my ____ res - cue. ____

And if I thought ____ our love ____ was
And I know that ____ this must ____ be

YOU ARE SO BEAUTIFUL

Words and Music by BILLY PRESTON
and BRUCE FISHER

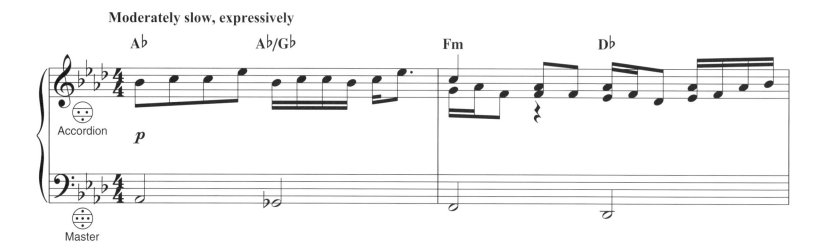

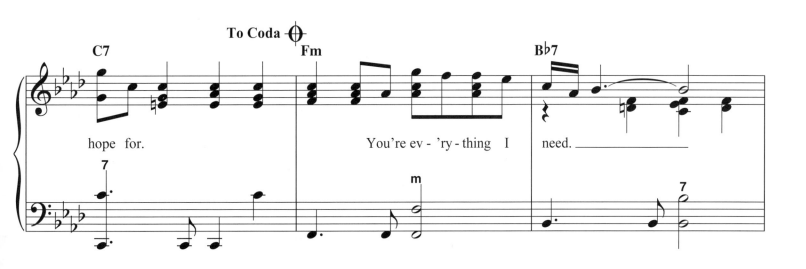

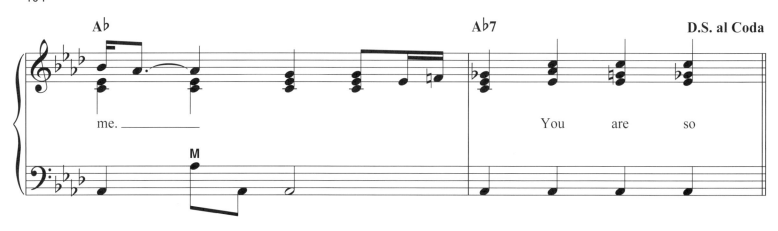

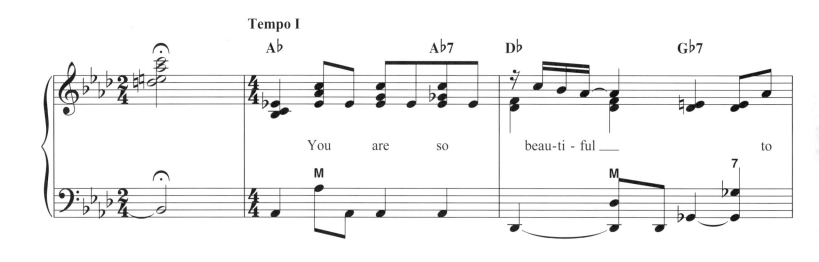

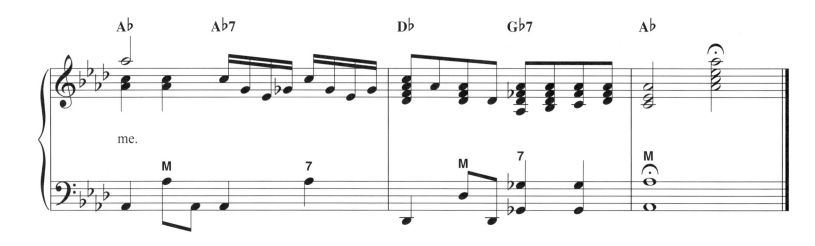